2413   OP 9L

DATE DUE

GAYLORD   PRINTED IN U.S.A.

Prison Writings

Prison
Writings

Régis Debray

Translated by Rosemary Sheed

Random House
New York

Library of Congress Cataloging in Publication Data

Debray, Régis.
Prison writings.
Includes bibliographical references.
1. Bolivia—Politics and government—1938–
—Addresses, essays, lectures. 2. Dialectical
materialism—Addresses, essays, lectures. 3. Debray,
Régis. I. Title.
F3326.D39713   1973   320.5   73–5101
ISBN O-394-48118-6

First American Edition

Contents

Political Writings

Theoretical Writings

Some Literary Reflections

Political Writings

Foreword

Political writings are by definition *ad hoc* writings, wholly conditioned by narrow considerations of time and place. Any awkwardness, any hesitation, anything that, given the wisdom of hindsight, can be seen as mistaken in the pieces reproduced here, must be put down to their having been written in the heat of the moment, and in conditions not conducive to academic tranquillity. This may leave them with so little of that 'greater dignity of the immediacy of reality', which Lenin attributed to the simplest essays in concrete analysis, as to make one wonder what interest there can still be in publishing them now. But, all things considered, they still retain enough of that modest and stumbling 'dignity' to precede what I have called 'theoretical' writings, in which the immediacy of reality tends to become blurred; and they certainly come far ahead of the subjective digressions – or regressions – which we call 'literary' because we must call them something, in which the immediacy of reality is woven into fantasies or word-spinning.

Lenin tells us that 'Marxism demands that we take account of objective circumstances and *how they may be modified*; questions must be asked in a concrete relation to those circumstances.' The circumstances we are concerned with here are those in Bolivia in the period of 1969–70, from the death of General Barrientos up to the advent of General Torres, and covering the government of General Ovando. From a European viewpoint, this strange game of military musical chairs may perhaps seem like one more wild piece of Latin American folklore, but to dismiss it as such would be a serious mistake. In point of fact, that period of Bolivia's history represents the final attempts of military reformism to provide an alternative to popular revolution; as that revolution developed it acted at once as its expression and its brake, an outlet and a side-track; and it presented the proletarian movement with delicate tactical problems going far back into the past of the International Workers' Movement; what then should be one's attitude towards bourgeois nationalism in an underdeveloped and semi-colonial country, in a period of dying imperialism?

That disturbed period was characterized by an extreme instability and uncertainty, a whirlwind development of events, and endless sudden and dramatic about-turns. In this book there are obvious contradictions as between one piece of writing and another, which are largely a reflection of the rapidity with which the situation changed, at a time when a few weeks might be long enough to produce a sharp change in tactics or judgement. To the extent that these pieces, hopeless as attempts at practical intervention represent attempts to seize the situation and follow the turning-points of history as closely as possible – though inevitably always a little behind (whereas a good politician should be prepared for them, even though he may be unable to take avoiding action) – the way they are written makes clear the material conditions in which I was writing, and how my work was bound *a priori* by those conditions to be at times inadequate, unbalanced or one-sided. I was in fact far from any urban centre and any direct source of news; there was censorship to be reckoned with; and I had no personal contact with the outside world.

A few chronological signposts should be noted:

☐ 27 April 1969: the accidental death of Barrientos. His vice-president, a civilian, Siles Salinas, took over as President of the Republic.

☐ 9 September 1969: murder in La Paz of Inti Peredo, leader of the ELN (National Liberation Army).

☐ 27 September 1969: Ovando, head of the Armed Forces, seized power in a *coup d'état*, and established a civilian-cum-military government in which, for the first time for many years, there was actually a 'left wing'. The government annulled the Oil Law, 'drawn up by foreign lawyers', restored the freedom of the trade unions, condemned neo-colonialism, and expressed a wish

to establish diplomatic relations with every country in the world.
□ 17 October 1969: chiefly at the instigation of the Minister of
Mines, Marcelo Quiroga Santa Cruz, the self-styled 'revolutionary' government decreed the nationalization of the Bolivian Gulf
Oil Company.

The piece which follows, 'Notes on the Political Situation', was
written a few days afterwards.

I Notes on the Political Situation in Bolivia[1]

1

The *coup d'état* of 27 September was at first, and for some days afterwards, greeted with widespread popular scepticism. Even the unexpected presence of a few progressive civilians, and the anti-imperialist tone of the government's first declarations, were hardly enough to stir the people out of their apathy and mistrust.

a) No programme of bourgeois democratic revolution would mean very much in Bolivia because a similar attempt had already taken place, and had ultimately failed simply because it was unable to get beyond its own initial limitations: that was the Revolution of 1952 which deteriorated so sadly afterwards. Yet, despite its ending in failure, the 1952 revolution had secured certain basic though limited victories: a petty bourgeois style agrarian reform, the (theoretical) integration of the peasants into the life of the nation and their right to vote, and the nationalization of the mines. That is why the comparison some people made with Peru seemed false. What gave the Peruvian military revolution its historical importance and its real content was precisely the absence of such a phase; hence the bourgeois democratic nature of that revolution did not prevent its playing a progressive role. It filled a void, a historical gap in Peru, that traditional bastion of the feudal oligarchy, the most colonial of all independent American countries. The very fact that it was so behindhand had the advantage of enabling the military government to declare a far more progressive agrarian reform than was achieved in Bolivia, directed to getting

1. Though written in October 1969 this piece first appeared in February 1971 in the Cuban Review, *Pensamiento Crítico*. It was then published in French in *La Nouvelle Critique*, in June 1970, and it is of this latter version that this is a translation.

rid of minifundism[1] and agrarian mini-capitalism with its backward and unproductive social consequences.

b) Another factor which makes it difficult to compare Bolivia with Peru is that the latter was far more developed industrially, in Lima and along the coast, and therefore had an industrial bourgeoisie which could support and profit from an anti-feudal and anti-imperialist revolution. In Bolivia, the lack of capitalist development had produced an unusually nervous and fearful national bourgeoisie, who felt no trust in their own strength, and were dependent both economically and ideologically upon imperialism.

As to the bureaucratic middle class, the major support of the ruling MNR,[2] its subordination and weakness and lack of any of the genuine bourgeois qualities were amply demonstrated. This inability to rule on the part of the industrial bourgeoisie and petty bourgeoisie can be seen all too clearly from the fact that they are still powerless to act themselves to defend their own economic interests on the political scene: they need the Army to enable them to wield power.

The 'middle class' showed itself unable to take its stand as an independent class against the oligarchy inside the country, let alone against imperialism, and preferred to vegetate in poverty under the protection of its supposed adversaries.

Certainly in this respect the situation has been modified since 1952, but essentially it has not changed. Bolivian capitalist development is concentrated chiefly in Santa Cruz, and it is no mere chance that 'the impudent company directors of Santa Cruz' have been the only group of people in the country to protest against the nationalization of Gulf Oil – from whose table they have been gathering the crumbs. It is worth studying the record of complaints

1. Ownership, as opposed to renting, by peasants of plots of land too small to provide means of independent support. The *minifundio* cannot exist apart from the *latifundio*.

2. Nationalist Revolutionary Movement, founded by Paz Estenssoro, Siles Suazo and Carlos Montenegro in 1941. It came to power in the popular rising of 9 April 1952, and retained control until 4 November 1964, when a coup led by Barrientos and Ovando forced Paz Estenssoro to flee to Lima.

from the National Chamber of Industry recently presented to the Minister of Labour, to gauge the gulf that divided the interests of developing Bolivian capitalism from any genuinely nationalist ideology.

2

It is at these two points that we can find the roots of the undoubted contrast which exists at present between Bolivia and Peru. Whereas in Peru bourgeois democratic activity can be described as revolutionary, since 1952 that has become an impossibility in Bolivia. A revolution in Bolivia – if we take the word in any serious sense – can no longer be led by the petty bourgeoisie and so-called national bourgeoisie because these (literally 'middle') classes have already played their role in history in the national revolution of 1952, and they have shown in practice during the past ten years that they are incapable of playing that historical role successfully – the role, that is, of building up the nation.

It is not surprising, then, that in the days following the coup, the old MNR cadres were enthusiastic over the civilian-cum-military junta. Though certainly it is inconceivable that there should be a profound revolution in *any* Latin American country that was not nationalist, not linked up with the past and the national tradition, that does not mean that every demonstration of nationalism is therefore revolutionary: everything depends on its class content.

When Augusto Céspedes,[1] whose intelligence and personality I admire enormously, tells us: 'Ovando is the new Busch;[2] may he have greater success than we had when we were young, and try to achieve the goal which our generation was unable to reach,' we

1. A well-known Bolivian novelist and political writer, author of *Sangre de Mestizos*, *El metal del Diablo*, *El Dictador suicida*, etc., a founder of the MNR and supporter of 'revolutionary nationalism'.
2. A nationalist Colonel, President of the Republic after the Chaco war, from 1937 to 1939, who finally committed suicide. He adopted the first anti-oligarchic measures to nationalize natural resources.

may wonder whether those who fought for popular nationalism in the past have learnt anything from history; whether the past thirty years have taught them anything, or indeed whether they have yet discovered the reasons for their failure.

Certainly the new intellectual and political generation has a greater fund of experience and a better knowledge of the turns and twists of the enemy, both inside and out; but that practical experience would be of no value if they could not learn the great central lesson of the immediate past: if the struggle for national liberation is to be consistent, it cannot set itself the same goals as it did in the days of Busch, and must therefore turn to other methods and other social moving-forces.

To these two reasons, which would occur to any revolutionary in view of what happened on 27 September, there must be added others, directly related to the forms of the new régime and obvious in the extreme, all of which militate against the 'revolutionary' coup:

☐ The fact that the takeover of power took the form of a putsch, and the anti-popular image of the army – an image imprinted in the living flesh of the people with special cruelty since the revolution to restore the *status quo ante*, and dramatically illustrated by the Barrientos repression, the murder of Che and, a few days before the coup, that of Inti Peredo. (It is also a fact that no one could disregard the nationalist military tradition represented by the names of Busch and Villaroel,[1] which, for all its fine words, had been so often made use of by the very men who had sold out. There was also the example of the Peruvian army: the lack of mass participation, and the illusion of having a 'revolution' imposed by the government through decrees and actions enforced from above on a subject people.)

☐ The devaluation and lack of credibility of all nationalist and revolutionary speeches, because of the inflated verbalism which such uses of language had undergone for so many years in Bolivia –

1. Nationalist Commandant, President of the Republic from 1943 until 1946, when he was overthrown by a popular rising, and hanged by the mob who supported the MNR.

a country second to none in Latin America in its experience of deception and disillusionment.

Of course, the fact that the junta had civilian as well as military members surprised a lot of people, but the reason for the participation of the civilians was not yet clear (and indeed is not wholly clear yet). The deeply entrenched traditions of Creole opportunism, and the fact that people had witnessed so many unlikely-seeming changes, did much to deaden the shock of seeing a few respected names on the list of ministers. The presence of Quiroga Santa Cruz, a man both intelligent and honest – two qualities almost never found in official political leaders, and which had in fact caused him only recently to be imprisoned under the Barrientos régime – was certainly a matter of great interest, but far from being clearly understood.

3

Faced with such a situation, what could one, what should one 'logically' expect? Here I am taking as read two theoretical premises which there is no scope to develop in these purely political notes. The first, a generalized theory, relates to the historical role of the bourgeoisie. We may recall what Engels said in his preface to the Italian edition of the Communist Manifesto: 'It is not possible for the bourgeoisie to rule in any country which has not got national independence.' However much of a caricature the Latin American – and especially the Bolivian – bourgeoisie may be, it remains that that bourgeoisie is looking forward to a time when it has power, and for it to have power a national state must be established. Weak and wishy-washy though it may be, that class can no longer bear being subject to North American imperialism; it can no longer grow and develop without first abolishing national dependence, and in this sense, there exists an out-and-out contradiction between it and imperialism. In the more developed countries of the sub-continent, Christian Democracy ('revolution in liberty') is the first attempt to resolve that contradiction, to pass from the status of a Yankee satellite State to that of a freely associated State, by seeking a different division of the plus-value as between the metropolitan country and itself. In the less developed countries, the response is neo-militarism (as in Peru and Bolivia). But that national bourgeoisie, or middle class, is also at enmity with the proletariat, as an opposing and threatening class. Hence it has to struggle on two fronts at once:

☐ on the one hand to get back its wealth, and above all its right to exploit the wealth of the nation for itself and its own profit – in other words, 'anti-imperialism';

☐ on the other, to defend its ambitions as an exploiting class against the working classes, to defend its ideological hegemony and its political positions – in other words, anti-communism, repression, 'rangers',[1] etc.

The situation is a paradoxical one, for this dominant class can only consolidate its domination by using the support of each of its opponents to conquer the other; that is to say, it needs a structural political and military imperialist support to cope with a possible armed struggle (thus needing military missions, weapons, the apparatus in Panama, instruction leaflets, and everything else the Organization of American States has to offer). But, on the other hand, to support its own rights as against imperialism, it needs to draw together all the mass forces into a single national anti-imperialist front. This could well explain its steps forwards and backwards, its duplicity, its traditional swings to right and left, etc. – at least in the abstract.

My second premise to be taken as read is that the Army, as an institution and a social force, represents not the interests of the oligarchy (especially in a country like Bolivia), but of the middle class as I have defined it. That means that in the least historically developed countries it falls to the Army to represent the economic and political interests of the group in the centre, caught between their two enemies – the outside, imperialist enemy, and the inside enemy, consisting of the proletariat, the poor peasants and the revolutionary intelligentsia.

1. American-trained counter-insurgency groups.

Again, we are talking in abstract terms. For, as we shall see, there are conditions in which this mechanism does not function. In a situation like the Bolivian one, there is no absolute certainty as to what will happen, which is important in a process like the one we are witnessing. Yet if we ever forget these *class determinations*, we may be courting grave shocks and disappointments.

With these two theoretical keys in hand, any observer could have foreseen the Ovando coup and its nationalist orientation. The programme, the composition of the government (including the presence of some of the most enlightened representatives of the 'national bourgeoisie', the civilians), even the nationalization of Gulf Oil, and establishment of diplomatic relations with socialist countries – all this was in the air, and especially so in that, as representing the tiny national bourgeoisie, the Army was being hard pressed on the right, towards imperialism, because of the anti-guerrilla struggle. Because of the blows it suffered from the left, the law of action and reaction had thrown it into the arms of the *Diario*,[1] the CIA, the Cuban counter-revolutionaries, and the forces of reaction at home and abroad. At the same time, it could only find itself again as a social and ideological body in tune with its class nature, by turning sharply to the left. Otherwise it would no longer have been of any use; it could no longer have played its historical role, which is to fill the central hollow between the two 'plateaux' of national forces. To shoot down miners and guerrillas was merely to waste ammunition. Ovando, a man whose intelligence one must never underestimate, had recognized this for a long time.

4

What then was there to fear? That advantage might be taken of the shock produced by the anti-imperialist measures to do away with workers' and students' organizations by taking action in the universities, decapitating and dividing the workers' movement, and

1. The leading extreme right-wing national paper, closely connected with the CIA and the American Embassy.

so on – none of which would have been possible in normal circumstances, but which might go relatively unnoticed in the euphoria of nationalization. Such at least had long been my own fear. In this way an anti-imperialist front would certainly have been established, but one wholly governed by the national bourgeoisie with its components powerless to express their views. After the coup against the right comes the coup against the left, the battle on two fronts, ideological confusionism, nationalist demagogy.

But basically events have not followed quite that course. One cannot say that the precise opposite has happened, but with the State security law on the watch, the promise that the siege of the mines would be raised, the granting of their freedom to the trade unions, as protest by the workers led to the abandonment of the plan for union regimentation, and the attempt at dialogue with both academics and workers, there are indications of a definite policy. Anti-communist hysteria seems to have vanished from the scene, nor is there any systematic persecution of politicians, though it is sad to note in some of the statements that have been put out a certain confusionist tendency to make simultaneous attacks on imperialism and 'Castroism', to sow discord and to fight on both sides at once as petty bourgeois rhetoric demands. (During the MNR period the slogan was, 'Neither with Moscow nor with Washington', and in Peronist days, people added, 'Nor with Buenos Aires'. Nowadays, there are those who say more aggressively still: 'We are against capitalism and against socialism.' With its slogan the MNR ended up in Washington, in other words in a state of nothingness: we may hope that those who are repeating these meaningless formulae today may have better luck. It would be far better once and for all to abandon these unreal problems, and state the real problems, straightforwardly and minus the demagogy.)

Recently a new element has appeared which might well prove decisive. It consists not in the nationalization of Gulf Oil in itself, but in the form in which it has been done and its political context. As we know, the national bourgeoisie and the company directors, in their limitless small-mindedness, have not supported this measure. But it was adopted unhesitatingly and speedily; in other words, the civilian-cum-military government identified with the most progressive popular demands and did not yield to pressure. This could mark a whole new dynamism. For in fact this step necessarily presupposes others, and if it follows such a line, the present government cannot fail to grow gradually away from its own class origins and closer to the people. So much for the political context.

5

If what took place yesterday on the occasion of the *Día de la Dignidad*[1] is consolidated, then the door will open to a genuinely revolutionary dialectic; a dialectic in which the government leadership and the mass of the people can gradually radicalize one another by continued interaction. If the government accepts and sets out to make contact with the masses, then it can learn much from them, and the masses will learn to trust it and give it their enthusiastic support. If the people can become the active agent of the changes being planned and not, as they usually are, merely their passive instrument; if the people can develop their own spontaneous activity; if they are associated in the revolutionary process taking place today – then the Armed Forces will no longer be set above them as 'guardians', looking upon them as minors whose interests need careful watching. This presupposes a change of ideology among even the most progressive sectors of the Armed Forces. It also means that a revolutionary dynamic *can* develop, though what concrete forms it will take we cannot yet predict.

Today the key point whereby the present government can be judged to be progressive or otherwise is not so much the measure, adopted by the Cabinet, as its decisiveness, and its ability to bring to an end the system of manipulating the masses by getting them mobilized into action. The question of how they are eventually to

1. Day of Dignity – a day of popular rejoicing over the nationalization of oil.

be organized is obviously premature, if not positively utopian. As the government is now and as things are at present, it does not yet appear on the horizon.

As for the form, the newest element (to judge from bits and pieces heard over the radio) is yesterday's meeting. But what I saw written in the paper *Presencia*[1] of the grotesque incidents which took place during the parade and in the Plaza Murillo with the DIC (Criminal Investigation Department) and the high command, leaves me with certain reservations about this particular novelty.

It is not just a matter of anecdotes. What is changing is a whole political style. For the first time since the early years of the national Revolution, a dialogue seems to have been established between the government and the masses. Contact has been made at the very point upon which the civilian-cum-military government's capacity to form genuine links with the masses basically depends; that will do far more than any written decrees or resolutions to determine the revolutionary nature of the régime. Up until yesterday, the Ovando government was one of enlightened despotism: everything *for* the people, nothing *with* the people. Historically, the enlightened despotism of Charles III represented the last trump card, the final effort by Spain to save its regime of domination in the West Indies. In general, such enlightened despotism usually marks the final stage in a régime of class domination before it enters its death throes; and it is of its nature to be ineffective, to produce paper reforms only. What is new – and we have yet to see whether it was a pure accident, or whether it has in fact brought in something different – is the fact that the presence of civilians with officers inside the government is more than just play-acting in which the civilians have walking-on parts.

If it has, then it might mean that the national group in the Armed Forces sees its opposition to the masses as secondary, and its opposition to imperialism as the main thing; and, further, that it is aware that it can do nothing, nor can it achieve even a tenth part of its programme without the active, intelligent and ideologically clear participation of the exploited classes, the trade unions, the

1. A right-wing, Catholic daily, owned by the church hierarchy.

students and the revolutionary intellectuals. For Ovando to have opened his gates and his balcony to these vanguard groups, with no restrictions laid upon their stated positions, is a novelty which the Peruvian military revolution has not yet achieved. It is a courageous act because it involves risk. If the régime seeks the support of the people, it runs the risk of getting it, and to some extent of having to identify with the people's own aspirations and their rejections of compromise.

If a general really wants to get rid of his reputation as a strong-arm man, he has to pay a very high price: he has genuinely got to stop being one. Is Ovando ready to pay that price? In his recent speeches, he has to some extent given up paternalistic rhetoric and the counter-revolutionary 'caudillismo' which are simply the sunny side of that shadow of passivity and alienation from which the peasant masses look up to their father, their patron, as the earthly embodiment of their father in heaven. He has demonstrated a degree of humility, and his government shows a marked sense of team spirit. In all this he has far outstripped Barrientos, at least as regards the official running of his government.

6

If we look beyond the present time to the conditions for revolutionary development, we come to the following conclusions: the very weaknesses of the bourgeoisie, the very fact that capitalism is so behindhand in the country, can be converted into more powerful motivating forces than in neighbouring Peru; even the reasons for scepticism can be converted into reasons for hope. If its own specific situation does not oblige a nationalist–bourgeois style military revolution in Bolivia to remain well behind the one in Peru, it is possible for it actually to be more advanced than Peru for this simple reason: a nationalist revolution in Bolivia cannot depend on either the bourgeoisie or the petty bourgeoisie alone, and therefore it can only be a revolution if it stops being bourgeois–democratic in style. The weakness of the national industrial bourgeoisie is an excellent thing, because its great dependence on anti-national imperialist forces prevents it giving consistent support to the development of nationalism. Thus, if the present régime does not want to do an about-face, it will of necessity have to draw more and more support from the lower classes, who have nothing to lose and everything to gain from a break with North American imperialism. It was no mere chance yesterday that it was actually the COB[1] which organized and stewarded the public demonstrations. Not only did the COB give the day its name, but also its whole style and inspiration, proving that the national interest can only be fully defended if the workers, in alliance with the revolutionary intellectuals, take over the leadership. The marked anxiety, and in some sectors, panic, shown by the mass media of the national capitalist bourgeoisie, following this elementary step, were no mere chance either.

As a student leader from Santa Cruz pointed out from the balcony of the Palacio Quemado,[2] at this level Ovando's team are laced with the alternative of either fulfilling the hopes their action has aroused among the people, whether intentionally or not, or of betraying them. It must be added that this government, if it is to be consistent with the image of itself which it has tried to present, will have to be inconsistent with itself in breaking the fetters of its class. If it wants to fulfil and achieve its own bourgeois democratic objectives, it will have to go further, and change into a popular government, with quite different content and methods.

Here we have the essence of the experience history has taught over the past twenty years: the failure of bourgeois reformism, whether in the populist form of the past, or the nationalist form of the present. What happened in Argentina with Perón, in Brazil with Vargas and Goulart, in Bolivia with Paz Estenssoro himself and the national Revolution, in Chile with Frei and his Christian Democrats – all these things demonstrate that a petty bourgeois or

1. The Bolivian Workers' Confederation, whose leader is Juan Lechín. It held its Fourth Congress in May 1970, under the Ovando government, adopting the fully socialist positions laid out in its Political Programme.
2. The presidential palace in La Paz.

populist régime, without any consistent ideology or conscious and self-regulating organization of the working classes, inevitably finds itself faced with this alternative: either it must move towards socialism, and manage to mobilize the masses on the basis of a programme of socializing the means of production (the land, industry, banking, foreign trade, etc.) and the State power itself; or, it remains enclosed within its original limitations and ends by being defeated – breaks with the people, sooner or later compromises with imperialism and is finally left hanging, with no effective popular support, and no defence against the counter-offensive of the oligarchy in alliance with the US. To refuse to choose between the two camps, to seek every means of avoiding commitment, means that it finds itself in a no-man's-land between the two, a no-man's-land which is a historical void. In any semicolonial and dependent country a middle position must sooner or later become a void since it bears no relation to the level of development of the productive forces, nor to any real hegemony or identification with the nation of the bourgeois class. The France of de Gaulle, in which these historical conditions were actually realized, could barely manage to hold such an intermediate position between opposing blocs at the political level. What might seem to a national bourgeois government like the present government of Bolivia, as the most prudent, wisest, most balanced position, represents in the long term the greatest imprudence, the most enormous risk.

The pity is that people generally only realize this too late. It is hard to stay sitting between two chairs for any length of time; politically, such exercises in levitation can only last for a few years. Populist rhetoric is as temporary a support as nationalist, and good intentions, sincerity, genuine and worthy patriotic emotion, can not in the long run substitute for social forces organized and guided by a scientific theory of social development.

This does not mean that all one need do to get out of being a satellite of the imperialist bloc is to become a satellite of the socialist bloc, as petty bourgeois propaganda would have us think. On the contrary, the only way a semi-colonial country can consolidate and build up its own independent national existence is to base itself on the solidarity of the socialist camp and the revolutionary movement all over the world. But the chief basis of support for a popular national régime must be the exploited classes at home, and at the international level, socialist countries and those countries which are immediate neighbours and/or subject to the same problems.

At home, the movement towards socialism means, among other things, fostering increased economic planning, which presupposes control of the major means of production by the State, promoting the best possible use of the most abundant of all factors of production – that capital which consists of the mass labour force – which presupposes that the people support and actively participate in the revolutionary process, and so on. These things have been said so often as to be almost clichés, and I would like to move on to the next point. But first, let us sum up what has been said so far: if the revolution is to be an out-and-out nationalist one, then it must not be a petty bourgeois one; and if it is to continue to be petty bourgeois in style, with all that that means, then it will have to abandon the claim to be nationalist.

7

What has begun in this country is obviously not a true revolutionary development, but a possibility. It is clear that a door has been opened. We cannot yet foresee what will go through that door, whether the civilian-cum-military government will cross the threshold or not. But they must be helped, urged forward, fuelled for the effort. And if they refuse to go forward, then our responsibilities will be clear.

Up to now the attitude of the popular forces has been beyond reproach, since, as a result of their many experiences, the national proletariat seem to have a remarkably high degree of class consciousness. Their attitude has been to reject the false and dangerous trap of being forced into choosing between a disdainful dissociation from the present government or unconditional and dependent submission to it. What matters is to preserve independence of class, of judgement, of organization. The experience of co-government during the MNR period was enough to show what disasters ultimately befall the working masses if they ally themselves with the petty bourgeoisie in power. The right attitude would seem to be that which the trade unions and universities are in practice adopting: one of critical and watchful support.

Enthusiasm is perfectly compatible with lucidity. Critical support may well be enthusiastic at times and even quite uncritical at vital moments, but it must always go hand in hand with ideological clarity and a precise awareness of the class nature of this or that political course, of the balance of forces existing among the classes in the country, and of the changes occurring in that balance as events unfold. A strong ideological and political struggle must be worked out against the illusions and hesitations of the petty bourgeoisie. Their mistakes, their failings, their faults must be criticized, and they must be saved from the explicit or implicit domination of imperialism – its newspapers and magazines, all its channels of ideological intimidation – and won over to the idea of a non-capitalist way of development. The immense layer of fears and lies which prevents people having a realistic understanding of the world-wide revolutionary movement, and the Cuban revolution in particular, must be swept away. All this work must be done by those who have the intellectual and material means to defend the positions of the proletariat and of socialism – that is, students, those engaged in intellectual work, together with the press, and activists in workers' parties and trade unions. Obviously all this ideological work can only be done in and through the daily political struggle, social action, and the defence of the economic interests of the people. This last point will soon become the major one as a vital consequence of the nationalization of Gulf Oil, which will cause huge financial and economic problems, and meet with reservations and a general counter-offensive by the national bourgeoisie.

8

In brief, what we must struggle for is the ideological hegemony of the popular forces over bourgeois forces, both inside and outside the country.

At present that hegemony is non-existent. As things develop, this situation can be made to change slowly but surely, but it is certainly not something to be achieved in a day. Every revolution is a development, and it would be wrong to dismiss this one as petty bourgeois, and withdraw into an ivory tower of Marxist–Leninism, leaving the battlefield and its manoeuvres to the rival groups of civil and military bourgeoisie. No; we must first struggle to impose our presence and active participation upon the present political terrain; and then, after that, to take over the leadership, not by any artificial means, but by proving that in the last analysis it is only the mass of the people who can make a popular revolution, determine its direction, and lead it. Revolution is a process. What matters is that conditions should so combine as to make it possible to set on foot a creative process, a revolutionary dynamic. Whatever happens, there will be a dynamic, and it will keep growing; depending on which forces have the greatest influence over it, the government may move left or right, but move it must. The law of .inertia does not apply to the mechanics of politics, and the role of our political organizations must be to cut off the route to the right and direct all movement the other way.

Perhaps the reader may consider my speaking here so insistently of alternatives, oppositions and antagonisms of class interests as either unrealistic or surprising or perhaps just the result of my being a foreigner.

Everyone agrees that the era of parties embodying selfish class interests is past, and that, taking the rough with the smooth, we must close our ranks, and establish a united anti-imperialist front. There may be others who say that there is no such stratification into separate classes in Bolivia, that it exists only in germ, unconsciously, and that once the real contradiction between the oligarchy and imperialism has been got rid of it may be found that there *are* no other really opposing interests.

9

Without going into this last analysis (though it is vital to get rid of the kind of pseudo-truths which help the petty bourgeoisie to defend their own leadership so well, pseudo-truths which play such a central role in the ideology of that class), let us get to the essential point. It is clear that in the present political situation, and indeed generally in the situation of any semi-colonial country fighting to achieve genuine liberation, all thinking and action must be in the context of a united front rather than of isolated class-determined parties – still less splinter groups. That front must include the petty bourgeoisie; but, above all in Bolivia because of its social characteristics and historical experiences, the petty bourgeoisie must not be allowed to become its guiding force. The rule must hold good against every temptation to opportunism, eclecticism or bureaucratism.

But there must be no question of fomenting divisions among classes and groups, for it is to the advantage of everyone to be in alliance. The future of the revolution, or rather perhaps the question of whether or not there can *be* a revolution, depends on the union of the urban petty bourgeoisie with the popular forces, the poor peasants, the proletariat, and revolutionary intellectuals.

It is important not to lose sight of the fact that, despite the individual presence in the government of certain (bourgeois) progressives, there are no representatives of the popular forces. It is the civil and military petty bourgeoisie who hold the power, and in general it is they who have in their hands the running and control of that united front. If this situation does not change, the revolutionary movement will rapidly stagnate. Union with the petty bourgeoisie: yes. Under their leadership: no.

The obstacles in our path are so many and so obvious that I need only mention the major ones: this short list may be a useful reminder. Temporary enthusiasm among the people, as great yesterday as was their frustration the day before, can at times make one lose sight even of what is most obvious.

a) The class nature of State power has not changed overnight, especially since the chief, and almost only, pillar of that State consists of the Armed Forces which brought about the change. The State apparatus remains intact. In this respect, the class nature of that apparatus is more evident in provincial towns and in the countryside than it is in the capital, where political comings and goings, and the shuffling of ministerial posts, provide a certain smoke-screen. Elsewhere the vertical and authoritarian structure of domination and control of the people remains precisely what it was. The newly-arrived lieutenant from Panama, the officials of the DIC, and other repressive bodies, make the law as they always did, manipulating 'their' peasants, 'their' *caciques*, so that the municipal administrative authorities are elected on their orders as always. This is a more deeply-rooted and dangerous phenomenon than any other, and one that cannot be changed by any written programme. And, speaking of written rules, what remains equally intact is the omnipresent newspaper and radio machine, designed systematically to misinform, under the control of those formidable agents of intellectual oppression and imperial deception known as the United Press, the Associated Press, and, to some extent, Reuters.

b) Though there is undeniably a progressive group within the Army, there is equally undeniably a movement of a very different kind.

The opposition is not just between two sectors of the Army; it also exists within every individual member of it. Though the Armed Forces present themselves in public as a homogeneous body, they cannot by doing so get rid of that internal struggle.

There is, furthermore, a marked reactionary paternalism in the behaviour and official views of the Armed Forces as an institution. They speak in the name of the people, and almost instead of them – so much so that they tend to see themselves, not as one more element associated with others in a popular national front, but as a kind of guardian angel, with a divine right to a position of un-deniable pre-eminence over all other categories of the popu-lation.

10

There is no re-making history. The line that ran from Toro[1] through Busch to Villaroel, even apart from its social and political aspects, is simply another side of the coin. Busch's suicide was not just a chance, any more than was the anti-national restoration put in hand by his successors, Generals Quintanilla and Penaranda (who were not forced to commit suicide). As for Villaroel, it was no secret that on 21 July 1946 he was abandoned and betrayed by all the garrisons in La Paz, and almost all his fellow-officers and leaders. Céspedes could tell us about the first point, and German Block Monroy about the second. There is no need to linger over what happened after 1946.

This ambiguous and obviously unfortunate fact that the Army is entrenched as a bourgeois institution, despite all the good in-tentions of this or that individual officer, despite any situation circumstances may create, is reflected on the international level. It is clear that at present the Ovando government is on the same side as the military government in Peru; we may talk of progressive officers, by contrast – in the context of Latin America – with colonialist–fascist officers, such as the anti-popular dictatorships in Brazil and Argentina. But one must not forget that none of these armies care much which side they are on, and all preserve the closest international relations. They continue their journeys, contacts, conferences, meetings, just as in the past, without there being the slightest crack in their defensive façade. Instinctive solidarity and tradition seem to be far stronger than political intentions, and it was no mere chance that the first to recognize the new government with obvious satisfaction were Brazil, Argentina, and Paraguay.

1. Colonel David Toro was President in 1936 and 1937, and was the first of the military presidents to suffer from 'nationalist' disquiet.

11

Now we come to the most important point of all: the neo-imperialist policy in Latin America. It is vital to avoid any simplistic interpretation, and to see North American imperialism for the complex thing it is. It would be ingenuous in the extreme to think that the mere nationalization of a few privately owned North American firms would provide US imperialism with a good enough reason to break off diplomatic relations. There are two factors involved: first, the Cuban experience, which taught the United States that overt economic aggression against a country on the road to emancipation can only precipitate its turning to socialism. This was something completely new and unprecedented, and could not have been foreseen in 1960; the Americans only recognized afterwards what a mistake their policy towards the Cuban revolution had been – their discontinuing of the sugar quota, refusal to refine oil, breaking off of diplomatic relations, and so on. These were all so many aggressive acts which only served to radicalize both the leadership and the masses in the country. In order to avoid provoking further Cubas, imperialism has long become resigned to sacrificing some of its economic interests in order to safeguard what the Pentagon sees as most essential: the continuance of its structural, political, and military domination of the nations in its backyard. That means being able to continue training Latin American officers in Panama and other military centres, to continue controlling arms sales, to carry on the aid and the military – technical missions unknown to public opinion, but omnipresent in every sphere, and, of course, to preserve the OAS, the BID (Bank for Inter-American Development), the World Bank, the Junta for Inter-American Defence, the Latin American bloc at the United Nations, and so on – in other words, all the basic organic structures of imperialist domination.

The second factor is not military but economic. The channels through which North America penetrates and dominates the sub-continent no longer depend solely on the classic specialist monopolies for exploiting raw materials – oil, copper, iron, bananas, coffee, etc. – but on conglomerates of international and more complex services – insurance companies, supermarkets, transport services, planning, and so on. This type of investment has less to fear from nationalization than from political instability, and we have seen no decrease in the total of Yankee investment over the past year. That total has amounted to some eleven thousand million dollars, with a profit rate of $12\frac{1}{2}$ per cent; and of course, as far as oil goes, the most recent discoveries in Alaska have brought the North American economy to the verge of being self-sufficient. Under these circumstances, the oil deposits lost to Gulf Oil in Santa Cruz really represent no more than a drop in the continental bucket.

12

In Latin America, and particularly in Bolivia now, the key to socialism lies in revolutionary nationalism. But the key to revolutionary nationalism in turn lies in socialism. It is up to the people of Bolivia to find their own forms, their own ways of travelling towards socialism, bearing in mind their traditions, their national character, their whole past and its values. Today there is no longer a model, a 'mother country' or universal centre of socialism. Every nation must discover and build its own individual road – though that does not mean that it should not learn from the experiences of other nations which have gone ahead or are moving alongside it.

And what such experience teaches is that no country can preserve its sovereignty or weld itself into a nation – whether it be the Vietnamese, the Cuban, or the Algerian nation – without seeking support from socialist and progressive forces all over the world. To become independent does not mean to become isolated. The question whether the revolutions of Peru and Bolivia (or the attempted revolution in Bolivia) are or are not integral parts of the Latin American and world-wide revolution can only be answered from within, not from outside. Their fate and their future depend on the answer. An exploited nation that wishes to stop being exploited by international capitalist imperialism and rediscover itself as a nation must, in its own individual way, unite with the supra-national cause of all the exploited nations and classes in the world. What happened in Czechoslovakia is a purely European tragedy, following on from the Second World War, and the post-war situation. However we assess it, its circumstances were quite different from those of the three under-developed continents, and especially from Latin America.

Another lesson to be learnt from the history of revolutions in our own time is this: there is no such thing as an irreversible victory. Nothing is ever won once and for all, nothing is ever secure. Even socialism, if it is not a continuing victory, a continuing rallying of forces, ceases to be what it is. And if this is true of the most profound, most transcendent victories of the proletariat when organized into vanguard bodies, and guided from the start by brilliant men in the light of the best Marxist–Leninist theory, how much truer is it (for many, many reasons) of the possible beginnings of political change of a national–bourgeois type resulting from a straightforward military coup. What people felt yesterday, the *Día de la Dignidad*, was something right and legitimate. General Ovando's speech, telling the nation of the nationalization of the imperialist Gulf Oil company, was an almost word-for-word repetition of another speech – the speech made by President Paz Estenssoro, in October 1952, seven months after 9 April, after a hard and bloody popular revolution, announcing the nationalization of the mines in the Campo Maria Barzola.[1] And that October could further be compared with 6 August 1925,[2] when a new era was also promised in similar terms, and it was also declared that the country would at last be emancipated

1. A place near the Cataví mines, christened after a working-class heroine killed in the fascist repression of the preceding years. The decree nationalizing the tin mines – Bolivia's greatest natural resource – was signed there.

2. The day when the political independence of the 'Alto Peru' was proclaimed and the new country named after Bolívar. It is a national holiday in Bolivia.

economically for good. But nothing is ever 'for good', and we have the history of Bolivia to prove it, cruelly at times.

Obviously history never repeats itself identically. In making these comparisons I want only to show that what has happened is good and promising. But the future remains unknown, and we shall only see what the present represents historically when that future comes. The step that has been taken will derive its meaning from the steps that follow it; any measure is worth no more than how it is carried out. The State now controls oil. And who will control the State, and in whose interest will the oil be sold, and who will ultimately control the world market in which the raw materials of hitherto underdeveloped nations become commodities?

A door has been opened. It is up to the people to determine what lies beyond it. There must be hope, vigilance, and determination.

Camiri, 21 October 1969

II Letter to the Federation of Press Workers of Bolivia

In April 1970, the recently formed Federation of Press Workers o, Bolivia held its Congress in the town of Cochabamba; during that congress a strongly-worded resolution was voted demanding amnesty for political prisoners, and especially the liberation of the 'Camiri prisoners'. At the same time, the workers' organizations that were coming back into being, and the entire student movement, ran an intensive campaign for such an amnesty, so that General Ovando was forced to state that he was willing to 're-consider the problem of Régis Debray and open an inquiry into the Camiri Case'. It is to this statement that allusion is made here; though intended solely to gain time, it confused the 'democratic' and 'progressive' circles still favourable to the government, and was taken at its face value by the journalists' trade union. It was possible, in connection with this matter of the Camiri trial rather than because of it, to help to unmask the real nature of the régime, whose demagogy was becoming ever more devoid of any meaning whatsoever.

This letter was intercepted by the censorship authorities of the military prison and never reached its intended recipients. What is published here is translated from a copy.

To the leaders and members of the FTBP
Semanario Prensa

Camiri, 3 May 1970

Comrades and colleagues,
Let me assure you of my deepest gratitude for the united demands you expressed at your recent Congress in favour of all political prisoners, and myself in particular. Your generosity was all the more valuable in that it came as a surprise and indeed a lesson.

A surprise, because the 'major newspapers' of this country, self-styled free, western and Christian, would not have led me to expect anything of the kind, having accustomed me to that monotonous series of insults with which their columns have been filled for the past three years – *La Presencia*, with its triumphant and blissfully senile pharisaism, *El Diario*, the spokesman of the North American embassy, *Los Tiempos*, speaking for the *caudillo*, and so many others.[1] And the one lesson I have learnt above all is this: your attitude has taught me not to confuse external appearances with the reality they may conceal or leave unsaid; not to confuse the alarming walls of 'the up-to-now impenetrable fortress of the anti-nationalist periodicals' as you call it, with the workers who are forced to sell their labour in order to live, and, like serfs of the pen, to defend the alien interests of their employers. That fortress is still intact (and I think we must not forget the fact), but at least we now know that if those whose energies at present support its daily defence should one day take control of the fruits of their labour, then these paralysing chains of bourgeois internationalism will be broken. This appalling monopoly of the organs of expression by the exploiters will then cease – this entire well-organized network which keeps the continental backyard of imperialism not merely uninformed but systematically misinformed, so that people are condemned to live an alien life as if it were their own, while what is most their own becomes alien – alienated, in fact – separated from themselves, as much as they are from their brothers in neighbouring countries, or further away in Vietnam or Cambodia. The day will then come when a Bolivian from the city will be able to be informed about what is really happening in Peru or Brazil, without having to trust what the UPI or the AP choose to tell him, in their distorted fashion, about those countries. A day will come when he can read about the struggles of the Cuban people elsewhere than in papers put out from Miami Beach or Washington; a day when he will no longer have to watch pictures of a GI giving a caramel to a Vietnamese child, which neglect to mention that the same GI has just burnt down his village and his home, with

1. The three papers named are the leading reactionary dailies in the country.

the child's parents and everyone else still living there; a day, finally, when the Latin American who wants to discover what is really happening in his own country, and what it means, will not have to study the European papers or the *New York Times*. Let us hope that day is not too far off, and you may be able to hasten its coming! Happy indeed will that day be when 'the neutral observer', the 'trustworthy diplomatic source' or the 'generally well-informed spokesman' – though always anonymous – who has so much to say in American cables can finally admit that he is actually speaking for the CIA or the State Department.

In addition to my gratitude and my hopes, may I also say a few more definite, more personal, and more political words. After all, all of us who live here, whether warders or prisoners, journalists or government officials, kindly humanists or angry men, we all share the same political situation and our lives are governed by it. It is not for me to give an opinion about that, but I can speak of the effects it has on a situation I know fairly well and have known for some time – the situation of political detainees. Now that you have taken an interest in this state of affairs, it is up to us to speak with the honesty that there must always be between those who share the same basic (anti-imperialist) position, even though they may differ as to methods, means or theories.

I believe that in a further demonstration of your concern, you have expressed 'satisfaction' over the statements of the President in regard to 'reviewing' the Camiri trial, and re-examining my own case. I have two questions, Comrades. I may be, and very likely am, misinformed, because of the situation in which I am living. I have never managed to see a single copy of *Prensa*. I am not allowed to receive any Bolivian visitors, and in fact for almost four months I haven't been able to talk to anyone, not even my lawyer, Dr Mendizabal, nor my relatives; the rules about visitors here are somewhat unusual. If I *am* the victim of a mis-understanding, then please forgive me.

1) My first question. The President's declaration about a re-examination was certainly interesting; it was intended to please,

and it would seem to have achieved its object. But what does it actually refer to? Just what does re-examining the case mean? When did it begin and when will it end? Perhaps writing and signing a decree of amnesty (or deportation, or whatever), a right restricted to the Executive Power, demands years of study, examination and re-examination, even given that there really is a will to undo what they call 'a legal and human error' – and an error still worse for those who are languishing in the Panóptico without any judicial action at all, for Loyola Guzman and others in the women's prison. Have they perhaps forgotten to distinguish between good intentions and fact (we should all have liked to settle this and all other matters peacefully)? Between a declaration stating that something is being set on foot and a statement intended to make people forget that nothing is in fact being set on foot at all, nor will be? Between sincerity and deception? In whose interest is it to sow illusions, with words for external consumption, leading people to believe that a change is being considered precisely so that no change need be made, and thus gaining time? When will people see whether there is something or nothing behind this kind of smokescreen, and when will they see for what purpose it is put up before people of good faith every three months or so in order to confuse them?

This is not a question of sociology or morals, nor am I trying, even by allusion, to pin-point individuals. It is a matter of un-covering once and for all an established power structure which is bound to continue in operation whatever may be the intentions of any particular man in office. The problem is not whether or not anyone *wants* to solve the problem of the political prisoners (to say nothing of the far more numerous prisoners of other kinds); the problem is whether or not the present régime will translate that wish into action. Perhaps it is not the same social group which ultimately makes the decision to release today as it was two years ago. Perhaps since nine months ago there has been a change in those who wield the real power from their position in Miraflores? Do the civilians in the military government, the so-called pro-gressives, really share the power, or are they merely a cover-up for the fact that that power has not really changed at all? Facts cannot be altered by disguising them or refusing to face them.

Ever since Karl Marx, it has been accepted that in social affairs we cannot judge men, political régimes or periods of history according to their idea of themselves, still less according to the idea they would like to give of themselves to others; it is necessary to distinguish between the stated principles and the underlying reality, between the invariably excellent intentions and the some- times less excellent actions, between theory and practice. Here the stated *wish* which we have to consider is that there should be no political prisoners. The official *theory* (which in fact contradicts that wish – but one contradiction more or less matters little) is that there are none: there are only common criminals in the hands of the law. This is precisely what the rulers of Santo Domingo, Guatemala and Brazil all say – by a curious coincidence. But the *fact*, as you know, is that there are political prisoners. Therefore, those who want to help to solve a real situation cannot applaud or support the official illusions or misrepresentations – however excellent their intentions; they must instead help the people, their readers, to see more clearly the difference between the seed of facts and the wind of words (in fact the people already see it because they are the ones who are suffering from it), to compare what actually happens in a political trial with the more or less distorted view of it held by those in power. Mystification must be replaced by de-mystification; complicity or servility, by what you have publicly and bravely determined to do in trying to examine your capacity for analysing the facts and for interpreting them, and place it at the service of truth and of the people.

Forgive me for these 'abstract' arguments: they are in point of fact anything but abstract. Very soon indeed you will see them as supremely concrete; a new situation will unexpectedly be presented by the government – a government whose official title is not 'constitutional' but 'revolutionary' – in all its crudity and urgency, a hard and real alternative between a lesser or greater disgrace, between a forced decision and a series of struggles whose consequences are incalculable, a situation in which the pompous statements made to evade, delay or subtly dissociate their authors from what is happening, will finally sound as empty as they are and be recognized for what they are worth – but they may perhaps cost a great deal, not just in this country but all over the world. The reality of the class struggle is hard and inescapable. As the recent history of your country shows only too well, and as you yourselves have analysed it in your Congress, those who want to pass over, conceal or delay it, hoping for tidy solutions or sowing false hopes, are only making that struggle ultimately harder and more inescapable. Comrades, do not let that be the part you play, either in this small and secondary problem of the revolutionary prisoners here (so secondary, that from the heights of ministerial chairs they virtually disappear from view), or in the other undoubtedly more serious problems which will determine the fate of your country, and especially that of the exploited masses.

2) That, then, is my first question. It should go without saying, but it is better to say it. I know that you *do* recognize it, but the same may not be true of those who, whether happily or unhappily, talk in terms of a supposed and always future 'review of the Camiri trial'. We must be very clear as to the ideas and the interests involved. The bourgeois have interminable and serious discussions, they lose themselves in the twistings and turnings of their justice, their laws, their complicated machinery of repression; they clothe their *de facto* domination with talk of law, with rules and judges, grand buildings and ceremonies; it is of the nature of their social function to wield power. Everyone knows the role of a class State and the function of its legal machinery, whether it be France, the United States or Bolivia; as you know, the class struggle has no frontiers. But it can never be part of a revolutionary's job, whether he be French, North American or Bolivian, to get involved in the pointless labyrinths of its 'legal system', since he rejects as wholly illegitimate the prevailing system of oppression 'by force of law and arms'. It is surely impossible, without abandoning every revolutionary ideal, every class posi-

tion, to beg the oppressors to use their power to set in motion their repressive or judicial apparatus in order to remedy 'a judicial error'. Why not simply ask them to hand over their weapons to the people, or the keys of their ministries to those they are exploiting? It is one thing to be forced to submit to those mechanisms of justification known as 'justice', but quite another to collaborate with this *de facto* power by accepting a benevolent character-part in play-acting of this kind. I may remind you that I purposely refused to choose a lawyer at the time of the so-called 'trial' of Camiri, demanding to undertake my own defence, and that it was then decided that I should not be allowed to say a single word throughout the course of the public deliberations; my refusal was ignored, and it was the 'judges' who took it upon themselves to appoint an official advocate. That I am now asking Dr Mendizabal to help me is not so as to initiate new proceedings, but to deal with my personal affairs, since I have no relatives living in the country, or friends who can visit me in Camiri. I may remind you also that, after my 'sentence', I refused to appeal to any 'higher tribunal'. If now those same people who imposed that 'sentence' through their institutions choose to set their machinery in motion again, of course no one can stop them. But to place any hope in such proceedings, or to let oneself be involved or morally affected or compromised by anything one's jailers may or may not argue, that is and will always be impossible.

In effect, the following are the alternatives: either the present régime is revolutionary as it claims, in which case it should not be unduly concerned over a sentence pronounced by a servant of the previous régime which it overthrew by force and swept away, any more than it is concerned over the laws, the legally constituted authorities, the articles of the Constitution in force on the morning of 27 September 1969 and the elected legislators who then supported it; the present régime merely continues to follow the same revolutionary instinct it followed that day, to trust in the infallible voice of the proletariat (if in fact they are really listening to it), it will take action to ensure that decrees and verdicts do not remain valid a moment longer than the dominating class which pronounced them remains dominant; no sentence shot from the mouth of any gun remains in force once another, more powerful or cleverer, gun has replaced it. In this case, there is nothing more to re-examine – it is an open and shut case with no need for heart-searching. Or, alternatively, the present régime, despite its claim to be revolutionary, is just as anti-revolutionary as the regime it has ousted (the reality always takes some time to show itself beneath its disguise, remember, in such cases). If so, then the condemned or detained revolutionaries must continue as in the past to refuse any voluntary participation in the play-acting of the currently victorious counter-revolution; they must not become compromised in the show put on by any ruling class, be it American, European or Asian, to make the prevailing oppression appear 'legal', untouchable, unquestionable and sacred.

In the first case (i.e. if it *is* revolutionary), the executive power, which has up till now been facing far more urgent tasks, or been preoccupied with temporary though time-consuming details, is returning to normal, and putting an end once and for all to this ridiculous situation whereby a few anti-imperialists in government posts are keeping in prison their own allies, their brothers in the same hard struggle. At last the authorities are attending to what they are being asked to do by all sections of the people about this small matter which has for so long unfortunately been forgotten: one more decree about the affair, which could be written and signed in a quarter of an hour at the next Cabinet meeting. Luckily it is a short and straightforward matter – for certainly we do not want to waste the time of our rulers which is undoubtedly limited (as I hope they realize). 'Time is money,' say the Americans; 'time is life' too.

In the second case (i.e. if the change is *not* a genuine revolution), it is no secret that revolutionary organizations, subdued by years of experience and sacrifice, will then have no recourse other than to fight the violence of the counter-revolution with whatever means seem most suitable – as they have done and will continue to do in all the dictatorships on this Continent, whether they are following new lines, or the old 'judicial', verbal, propagandist procedures of the past, or whatever.

To imagine that there can be a third way, a middle or mediating way, is to enter a blind alley and play into the hands of those who want to make us do just that. It shows a failure in understanding, a fear of shouldering our responsibilities, and a lack of preparation for the bitter and sudden awakenings that lie ahead.

Thus, just as no one should confuse his feelings of impatience with a theoretical argument, neither should he confuse his dreams of conciliation with reality, nor his long-suffering or passivity with principles of action. The first is 'left-wing opportunism', the second, 'right-wing opportunism'.

But these are terms from Marxist–Leninist ideology and, because this government has rejected all links with the working class and with socialism, you may say that they are out of place. Since they call me an intellectual or an ideologue, and since there seem to be plenty of intellectuals and ideologues in this government which we may thus call 'bourgeois–democratic' – let them, if they want to understand better what I am trying to say here, refer to Jean-Jacques Rousseau, the father of all bourgeois democracies, when they were still young and hopeful, and to what he wrote in the *Social Contract*, Book 1, Chapter 3, about 'the law of the strongest' and its weakness: it is only one page, but very instructive and supremely relevant now, though perhaps somewhat subversive. It would be interesting to see how the present censorship would treat this agitator. Speaking for myself, I would not dare to quote him in the circumstances.

Don't worry, comrades and colleagues. You need not think that this letter will do any harm to the prisoners, or that it will give much pleasure to those 'who are preventing the amnesty', by providing them with any *corpus delicti*, any cause for life imprisonment. 'How can they set such an insolent creature free?' Comrades, we must be serious. For these people, a revolutionary who sticks to his guns, whatever his nationality, sex, state or profession is and always will be insolent, a danger, an enemy. They will call him a blackmailer and a rabble-rouser, as well as a criminal, a thief and a foreigner: I have learnt all these descriptions by heart over the past three years. Yesterday, 23 December,[1] they made an excuse so that I got no messages or letters from anyone, today they will make another, tomorrow yet another, and who knows how long it will go on? It may be that from the first we have all, from last October until January of this year, been deluding ourselves as to the present political trial, because such illusions then reflected what were objective possibilities that this government might become a popular one (though I would not go so far as to use the term 'socialist'). At that time, amnesty was not just an illusory dream. Up to then, while American imperialism was the major common enemy, it seemed that those working for socialism, and those who would define themselves as revolutionary nationalists, understood one another; they were travelling along parallel roads, without interference or enmity, though each from their own positions and each bearing their own banners. The passage of time does not seem to have sanctioned this view of things, and it may be that the moment has come to act upon the fact. I don't want to embark on an analysis of the present situation; it is not my business to do so, and in any case it is something that the most varied sectors of the Bolivian people are well aware of, as can be seen from the resolutions of the last Miners' Congress as well as those of the present COB Congress, to say nothing of the statement they approved in their last Congress in Cochabamba.

All I would say, as might any observer, is that those who still hold to the illusions of yesterday can be basically divided into two groups. The first, those childish people on the right, who justify their position by talking so much about the childish people on the left; everyone knows that the latter, if they deserve such a description, and even supposing that those who apply it to them are right, are very few in number, and abominably persecuted by the former from their position of power; they are immensely self-sacrificing, and learnt long ago to be intelligently Leninist, like Che and his comrades. The second group are the unwilling

1. In 'normal' times in Bolivia, it is customary to release all political prisoners on Christmas Eve every year.

accomplices or ideological victims of those in power, who play on their good faith. The child-like rightists, 'progressive' civilians and ministers, continue to hold and foster their fading illusions about the 'great national anti-imperialist front', 'popular participation', 'intensifying the revolution', etc. – indeed that is their one and only task – until those who have given them this propaganda mission send them packing because they are altogether too enthusiastic or ingenuous. For when those entrusted with the public relations of any enterprise come to believe in what they are saying, and to take as fact what they put out for public consumption, there comes a time when they are a danger to their own patrons, who always prefer the astute to the credulous for such work. As for the lower-ranking innocents, those who want at all cost to avoid the risk of a traditional restoration, they will have their eyes opened very soon, if they have not already, to the realization that you cannot change the direction the train is taking by jumping about in the rear carriage, and that the rails stay where they are despite all their good intentions, warnings, speeches or efforts, and lead inexorably to the very restoration they want to escape from. There is only one way to change the direction of a train: to take control of the locomotive.

I hope you will forgive me for having taken up so much time with this apparent hair-splitting which may sound more like a moral tale than history proper. I hope it may show the way towards certain basic principles or criteria which are applicable to other areas in the historical process.

Let me repeat once again my deep and heartfelt gratitude for your solidarity and solicitude. If you consider them suitable, it may be that you will find a corner in your journal for these words of mine – for I know that it is free, independent and spirited.

Fraternally,

Régis Debray

III Some Answers to Questions about a Failed Uprising

In October 1970, there was a further turning-point in Bolivia, far more dramatic, and indeed within an ace of being absolutely decisive: the 7 October quasi-rising of the masses in La Paz, against a junta of fascist officers (Miranda, Guachalla, Satori) who had suddenly, and briefly, established themselves in the presidential palace. The junta lasted no more than a few hours, and the tremendous mobilization of the people led to a compromise solution being reached between the still powerful Armed Forces on the one side and the trade unions and democratic parties on the other. That solution entailed the coming to power of General Torres and a régime considerably to the left of Ovando's, but lacking any organic basis of support apart from the Armed Forces.

The bloody repression of the guerrilla movement of Teoponte, a series of mysterious massacres and murders, the resignation of the last 'left-wing' civilian ministers, ever more obvious yielding to pressures and blackmail from international bodies and American imperialism, combined with the forces of reaction inside the country – all these together succeeded in a matter of months in making clear the instability of the Ovando government and its so-called revolutionary plans. This was the moment chosen by military reactionaries to bring him down, to force Ovando to resign and put their own representatives directly in his place, as during the days of Barrientos. The COB – which had just been reorganized and held its national Congress – then called for a national general strike, and this took place; the left-wing parties, in agreement with the unions, formed the Comando Político de los Trabajadores y del Pueblo – *from which the Popular Assembly under Torres was to be constituted – representing all the political anti-fascist and anti-imperialist forces, and providing leadership for the popular camp, while General Torres, from the Air Base of El Alto where he had taken refuge, gathered together all the civilian and military groups determined to resist the fascist coup. Fighting was particularly fierce at Oruro, the traditional bastion of the miners, where civilians and troops were in confrontation. In La Paz, the seat of political power, the rebel garrisons and the junta itself, caught unawares by the popular response, and ill-prepared for an armed confrontation, fled, leaving the presidential chair to General Torres. The crisis seemed settled. And yet . . .*

Only a few days after all this, a journalist got a questionnaire through to the military prison in Camiri – where the garrison had supported the fascist coup from the very first. The piece I reproduce here contains the written answers to the written questions, on the basis of the little information then available to us from such newspapers as we were allowed to read in prison. Since it remained in my cell for so long, it has not been published before.

Camiri, October 1970

Q. What do you think of the recent changes in Bolivia?
A. In brief, that they do not represent any profound change in the prevailing structure of power. We may say that in the good old game of see-saw, a nationalist and relatively liberal section of the military bourgeoisie is at present on top, with the other section acting as a counter-balance. This latter, the colonial–fascist section, has thus temporarily disappeared from view, but since its power remains intact, it will come up again the moment it considers it useful.

If one delves a little below the surface of the supposed 'changes', one soon sees that General Torres is not, as everyone says, the man who defeated the right, but rather the man who saved the right from political, and indeed physical destruction. He acted as a kind of dam preventing the water from overflowing, when, on 6 October, a genuine insurrection of the people seemed to be boiling up in the big cities, particularly La Paz. He held it back with great skill, taking the lead so as to be in a position to stop it, and deflect it into becoming no more than a short-lived reformist compromise. I think it true to say that the popular forces simply did not have the time to take direct charge themselves of the once-for-all overthrow of the leaders of the coup. Hence, it is not too much to say that the grotesque, pathetic, positively ludicrous nature of the puppet junta brought to power after Ovando's resignation by Miranda and the American Embassy represented a real misfortune. Had they succeeded in remaining in power for only a few more days, the whole people would have taken up arms, destroyed the most reactionary sections of the army, and thus taken their fate into their own hands – in company with (and why not?) the populist sections of the Army, and indeed General Torres himself, though not under his sole leadership. Though given the bloodshed that has in fact been saved, they may congratulate themselves on the relative peacefulness of the 'change' (despite the numbers of workers and students killed in Oruro), but if one thinks in the long term, it is clear that we shall be paying a high price in blood and lives for the hastily-formed alliance among the various sections of the Army which prevented the uprising. At that time, the balance of forces was such – thanks to the mobilization of the masses, the alliance between so many of the peasants and proletarians, the moral collapse of the fascists, the fact that a considerable section of the Army had been neutralized, the general though disorganized strike action, and the combative attitude of the popular vanguards, to name but some of the elements involved – that the cost of an armed confrontation would then have been minimal. Certainly far less than what it may, indeed what it must be in the future, in less propitious circumstances.

Of course the ' misfortune ' I am speaking of – the precipitate and abrupt way in which events apparently broke free – was no mere chance. It was knowingly planned and organized by the rival factions of the Army. The mirage of another 9 April [the rising of 1952 in which the oligarchy's army was swept away] appeared so suddenly and forcefully that both sections of the Army were terrified, and preferred a quiet reconciliation to a formal victory by the 'Torres group', which its opponents would have had to accept willy-nilly. This explains the last-minute alliance between the fascist junta and the Torres forces, and the latter's decision to support the members of the coup in what they had done, including the election of Reque Terrán as Commander-in-Chief as a kind of guarantee for the Right – all of which was done behind the backs of the people. They realized that they were playing with fire, and they therefore hastened to bring the game to an end; and when 7 October dawned, Torres was already in the Palace on the basis of a supposed popular victory. In fact there had been nothing but a clever imitation of a popular revolution – but by then it was too late to change the course of events. 'There are no victors and no vanquished' was the slogan launched inside the Army, and passed on to every garrison in the country; while outside, for the crowds gathered in front of the Palace, it was described with a wealth of rhetoric as 'the victory of the people over their reactionary enemies'. Of the two phrases, it was unfortunately the first which was true. The right wing agreed to sacrifice some of its most visible, most obviously compromised heads, in exchange for what was basically a preservation of the structure. Or, if you like, it had a finger or two cut off so as to save both its arms; a case of choosing the lesser of two evils. The great 'rout' of fascism thus richly deserves to be known by the military euphemism of a 'strategic withdrawal', though Torres, the supposed victor, concealed it with a torrent of fine words. In short, good old South American jiggery-pokery. But the people of Bolivia are not deluded by all this, and there is no doubt that they will go on working harder than ever for their ascent to power. And that ascent, through the work of politicizing, organizing and preparing the people, must be, and is continuing; indeed it is advancing by leaps and bounds. The Torres government is only the ground floor, and it does not look like lasting for long.

Q. How important, do you think, are the divisions existing within the Bolivian Armed Forces, which recent events have brought into the open? What effects may they have, in your view, on the revolutionary movement?

A. Obviously there are contradictions, and no revolutionary should (in my personal opinion) treat them as unimportant. But to know what attitude to take towards them, one must first analyse them, and consider just what form of contradiction they involve.

Sharp as they may appear in the circumstances – and leaving aside the exceptional instances of officials who would as individuals be prepared to fight with and for the people – these contradictions are, I believe, no more than secondary: in other words, whenever the popular forces burst onto the scene and look like endangering the Army's monopoly of using armed force, they will disappear. It is then that the *major* contradiction again comes to the fore, the opposition between the Army and the popular forces, both of which are fundamentally organized in view of their own class interests, and fighting for their own, socialist, objectives. Instantly then, the divided factions in the army reunite to escape and deal with the greater danger threatening it from below. The reunification takes place in the name of 'the sacred unity of the Institution' – Institution and Nation, of course, are one and the same thing – and it takes place whenever there is a hint of a popular militia coming forward, in an elemental instinct of self-defence and survival. The militia, the people in arms – that is the intolerable, the inconceivable nightmare; and in Bolivia it is a nightmare with a real, practical and quite recent existence, ever since the revolution of 1952. The more nationalist, the more 'open' a military leader is, the sooner he again becomes the brother of the most fascist of his 'comrades in arms', the moment he sees miners organized into armed detachments, or even glimpses such a possibility. And the re-mobilization of the workers' militias is not just a pipe-dream, a phrase to be bandied about in street-corner conversations; it is a wish for class organization, an immediate demand, the touchstone of every popular programme; indeed it figures among the twenty proposals or conditions laid down in the 'Mandato popular' presented to General Torres. No rhetoric, no juggling with words over the much-used term 'revolution', can long conceal this basic conflict of interests.

Recent events have made it clear that the conflicts existing within the army are not really antagonistic. No one military faction disappeared beneath any other, no officer fell victim to any other. Threats, alarming proclamations, troop movements, air displays, hedge-hopping flights – the lot, but actual shooting, no. As in Argentina (with the 'blues' and 'reds') there are positions to be gained, then accounts to be settled, and finally everyone sits at the negotiating table for the necessary reconciliation. But one Division, the Second, stationed in Oruro, carried out a massacre of civilian demonstrators, and the only result was that the government relieved its commander of his post. In short, the real victims of the struggle between the two military groups are to be found not among the soldiers but the civilians, students and workers. The conflict with them, by tradition, and thanks to the objective demands of class interests, is certainly genuinely antagonistic, and it puts the army as a bloc against the bloc made up of the proletariat and its allies.

But having said that, it would be foolish to take no account of the conflicts within the army; they should be studied with the closest attention. Only a childish sectarianism (christened 'gauchisme' by Lenin), or a metaphysical, moralistic, idealistic concept of the class struggle, refuses to recognize and ultimately take advantage of the enemy's secondary conflicts. It would be dangerous, indeed deadly idiocy to reject the possible help of valuable allies whenever and wherever they may be found; they may be won over first pragmatically and later perhaps ideologically, in the dynamic process of a complex, many-sided struggle, involving the traditional or institutional tendencies that might influence them, and draw them on to our own ground. And here I think it important to warn against a certain almost mystical or even religious, Manichean, concept of the political struggle, which applies even to its most intense and – in Bolivia unavoidable – expression: the armed struggle. You cannot abstract the concrete social forces as they are today, condemn them *en bloc* as 'corrupt', and withdraw from the whole thing. From the point at which the masses stand, from their present level of consciousness, their material needs, which though immediate can also be immediately changed, you cannot hope to set up a 'pure' and immaculate struggle, with no dangerous compromises, as against an established order that is impure, reactionary and utterly to be condemned in every respect. The moral notions of an enlightened vanguard are one thing; the class struggle which must set in motion hundreds of thousands of oppressed people, oppressed by their whole inheritance from the past, with all the failings and inadequacies of a capitalist, if not feudal history, or even of the primitive community, that is quite another. Men make history, but they do it on a foundation of previous conditions – not of their choosing, conditions from which they have to start precisely in order to be able to overcome them. Leninism made use of these generalized doctrines of Marxism in order to provide concrete solutions to concrete political situations, and 'the art of carrying on the political struggle in concrete reality', on a scientific basis, demands that we take into account the secondary conflicts of the enemy as much in order to turn them against him as to distinguish between strategic plans and tactical needs. The experience of the international revolutionary movement, from Lenin to Mao Tse-tung and Fidel Castro, gives a wealth of examples, or rather lessons, in this regard, which I need not enumerate here.

What *must* be emphasized here is this: we already know that those who are failing the armed miners, the groups of peasants taking over the land of the large proprietors for themselves, and the guerrillas in the hills, are not Miranda, Torres, Guachalla or Fulano, but those who represent the bourgeois system, 'to preserve private property against chaos and anarchy, etc. etc.', whose reactions are fundamentally the same. But we can discover what attitude to adopt from examining the actual nature of the conflicts existing in military officialdom. We must not attribute any *strategic* importance to them, in that they do not constitute the central axis upon which all the struggles revolve, nor does any section of the army constitute the possible support for a popular movement. It would be ridiculous to allow the future or the possibilities of success to rest on what this or that general or group of officers might decide. But what we must attribute to them is a great *tactical* importance, in the sense that the nationalist concerns, and populist inclinations of one section of the Army might, in certain circumstances, provide better conditions for a victorious popular uprising. They contribute to neutralizing a section of the State's apparatus of repression, to isolating and weakening its most reactionary elements, to establishing an unexpected breach through which the popular armed vanguards could break and seize political power, whether by means of a sharp, decisive attack, or a more lengthy struggle.

But such a proceeding can only take place, and can certainly only be sure of success, if the proletariat takes the principal and leading role, through its single union organization and its political organizations – and that is just what did not happen in the last crisis, although it was not far off. Up to now, the latent division within the Armed Forces has always been healed by their own efforts, at the last moment, with power swinging from one side to the other, from Barrientos to Ovando, from Miranda to Torres. Henceforth it will be a matter not of the people's taking power, either by force or by passive acceptance on their part, from one military section rather than another, but of seizing power from both groups at once. When I say 'power', what I mean ultimately is the power of decision, in other words the leadership; this does not by any means exclude the possibility of alliances, collaboration or unity of action with the anti-imperialist sector of the Armed Forces *under the leadership* of a solid popular front with its own armed organization. But as long as the Armed Forces as at present constituted are, or remain, in a position to make the supreme decisions, no coherent revolutionary process can take place in this country, there can be no guarantee for the popular forces, even as regards their physical safety. Of this the masses are well aware.

As far as an alliance with a relatively large section of the Army goes, it is not impossible, especially in the heat of the struggle; it might be a passive alliance of neutralization, or an active one of integrating military nuclei into the popular forces. I think it is a mistake to interpret the relationship between the people and the army in a static or monolithic way. In the dynamics of a revolution, the combination of a general uprising in the cities, rebellion in various parts of the country, especially in Oruro, in the mines and in La Paz, with a favourable peasant movement in other areas, might cause a large part of the Army or other repressive forces to hesitate. And, furthermore, it is worth noting the difference between high- and low-ranking officers, NCOs, private soldiers, and mercenaries, who are especially hardened and untrustworthy. In any case, it is very useful to re-read what Lenin had to say after the 1905 revolution about the Army and working with the Army. Lenin stressed that one must continually 'work' politically and ideologically with the troops, try to win over as many of them as possible, distinguish carefully between high-ranking officers and the rest, and, during an insurrection, try to surround the repressive detachments with large numbers of people, and immobilize them, subjecting them to massive pressure; he says that it may even be possible to win over a whole battalion by making them feel themselves outnumbered – if need be by the military method of firing a few shots. Let us also think well of that famous sentence in his *Account of the 1905 Revolution*: 'The history of the Russian revolution, like that of the Paris Commune, teaches us one incontestable lesson: militarism can never and in no circumstances be conquered and destroyed except by the victorious fight of one part of the national Army against the other.' Undoubtedly it is questionable whether that is *absolutely* true, in the light of some of the events of this century – especially in semi-colonial countries where the Army cannot always be described as 'national'. But it remains generally valid, especially in the case of Bolivia. Indeed, without recourse to Lenin, or any other distant or long-past experiences, it is enough to study the history of Bolivia itself, and its own traditions of struggle. Indeed, we need go no further than what happened here on 9 April 1952, when, within three days, the oligarchy collapsed before the Army.

In effect, the absolute dedication of all soldiers, whether they be reformists or fascists, to preserving the 'sacred unity of the

Armed Forces' constitutes the barrier which prevents any possible
revolutionary developments being begun within the Armed Forces.
This is the key problem, the touchstone, the stumbling block
which the 'revolutionary nationalism' of the troops will have sooner
or later to come up against; this is what hampers their union with
the masses, for the simple reason that such a union would necessarily involve an open and irreversible break with the fascist
section (that is, the majority) of the Army. For that reason, as
long as there has been no open rift in the military establishment,
as long as the imperialist, rightist officers who support the coup
have not been removed and relieved of their duties, it is impossible
to conceive of any plausible alliance between the working class on
the one hand, and 'progressive' soldiers on the other. And one
cannot expect soldiers formed – or malformed – from their
adolescence by the reactionary myths of the military academies to
destroy the very bourgeois establishment in which they have been
brought up and have made their careers. It is inconceivable for
them, and equally so for Ovando or Torres, who instinctively put
the interests of their own caste solidarity before that of the people
and their solidarity ; when faced with the inevitable dilemma, the
choice between unity with the people or unity with the establishment, they cannot help opting for the second. The spine of the
oppressor bourgeois State, which today in Bolivia is the Army,
must be broken; but that is hardly a job that can be entrusted to
the bourgeois Army itself, since no one can be expected willingly
to commit suicide. However, the Army as a bourgeois and oppres-
sive institution and 'guarantee of the established order' will have
to commit suicide, and be re-born from its own ashes as a popular
institution wholeheartedly dedicated to serving the people, the
workers, if it is, as such, to fulfil a progressive role in history.
And, in Bolivia, to fulfil a progressive role means, unquestionably,
in the circumstances now prevailing, and in the light both of
recent history and of the class-structure, to establish the bases of
socialism. Strictly speaking, in any case, a 'progressive', 'nationalist–revolutionary' soldier can only call himself a revolutionary
in the present situation if he is ready to consider those of his

'comrades-in-arms' who are on the other side as his enemies, and ready to accept the contradictions in his own life without being frightened to carry them to their logical conclusion – an open and honest and unhesitating break with the whole corrupt body of the oppressing Army. However good his intentions, any soldier who puts his professional establishment before his class situation, his caste-instinct ahead of his revolutionary instinct, will be forced sooner or later into a counter-revolutionary and anti-popular role. This statement is not just my dogmatic prejudice, my *a priori* conviction, my principle as an anti-militarist; it is a conclusion drawn from what we have experienced in Bolivia, the concrete facts of the case. It is a straightforward statement applying not to Chile or Peru, but to Bolivia.

In Chile, for instance, the military dogma of the 'rigid unity of the Establishment' plays an objectively anti-fascist, anti-coup role, because of the legalist traditions of the Chilean Army, the strength of the civil power, and the fact that the Army has traditionally been subject to the apparatus of the constitution. In Peru, the level of the class struggle taking hold there is not such as to render impossible a *via media*, a compromise between opposing interests on the basis of a prudent though continuing reformism, none of which would provoke serious upheavals within the Armed Forces. Furthermore, in neither of these countries does the Army have the experience of having been physically routed by the people; this has been a recent experience leaving fearful memories, and something of a permanent obsession, in the Bolivian Army since 1952. In Bolivia, the basic dogma of the unity of the Armed Forces, which must at all costs be preserved, come what may, as a guarantee of its 'physical and moral integrity', is something shared by both factions of the Army, and thus plays an objective counter-revolutionary, pro-fascist, pro-coup role. In fact, the right-wing *gorila*,[1] though he would not care a straw if that unity

1. *Gorila* (literally meaning 'gorilla') is normally used in many parts of Latin America to mean the high-ranking officers in right-wing military governments; it is sometimes used by extension to refer to other officers and soldiers fighting on behalf of such governments, and very occasionally to the police as well.

were broken in order to create a coup – against Ovando in the past or Torres in the future – uses the sacred cow of 'military unity' to protect himself, in order to preserve and strengthen his position should it ever be threatened. Indeed, not only are the Armed Forces as such actually the sole arbitrator, the supreme judge of every 'democratic opening' (Ovando first, and now Torres), even when there appears some kind of civilian–military alliance with the participation of a few naïve reformist intellectuals, or the complicity of astutely 'apolitical' professional men; not only do they decide in the last instance what the wretched ministers can or ought to do, but even inside the Armed Forces, thanks to the sacred dogma of unity, it is the *gorila* who becomes the arbiter, the final judge, of what the Armed Forces themselves can or should do. By means of pressure, blackmail about the 'unshakable unity of the Institution', veiled threats of open conspiracies, these fanatics finish by paralysing every reformist wish of the 'comrades' in power. The man who is supposed to be their agent ends by being their hostage, tacitly obeying all the commands of the ultra-rightists, until they consider it preferable to remove him from the presidential chair altogether, taking from him the attributes and appearances of power, and the title of 'His Excellency' in accord with the reality of the power already wielded by themselves. Ovando fell officially in October, but since July he had been no more than a figure-head, and as long ago as February he had capitulated unconditionally to the *gorilas*: having been faced by his 'colleagues in the High Command' with the alternative of expelling from the cabinet a few civilian agitators and 'demagogues' or disrupting the unity and mutual understanding between himself and the military leaders, he naturally chose the first. The risk was smaller. And Torres capitulated on the very day he took power: presented by two or three leading regiments with the choice of letting the people take a large share in his government and having then to deal with his highly-placed 'colleagues', or removing the workers from all political power and thus achieving a peaceful coexistence with the Armed Forces as a body, he naturally chose the second. Nor did he realize, as was also natural, that he was thus sealing his own failure as a 'revolutionary', and indeed, ultimately, as a ruler. Bolivia today is a sad country, for it is a country where there must be drastic, urgent and speedy definitions, and yet the wish to avoid making them makes them ever harder to make. To play tricks with history may be clever; but it is bravery and decision that are the best stratagems now. In this country, the time for cleverness is past.

One comment here. I happened to see the paper *Presencia* for 8 October, with a piece on the first page giving a tremendously clear picture of the best way to frustrate 'revolutionary nationalism' in the Bolivian military manner. I need do no more than quote it. The headline was: 'Officers of the General Headquarters [i.e. the coup-planning *gorilas*] state: We have presented our view as to how to achieve the unity of the Armed Forces.' The text is as follows:

To seek the unity of the Armed Forces, to achieve public calm and recover from the crisis situation which has spread through the country – these were the bases agreed at a meeting between representatives of the commanders and officers of the Headquarters of Miraflores and the new revolutionary government led by General Torres ... Colonel Miguel Ayoroa declared that he had reached a compromise with General Torres who, he said, in a generous spirit, guaranteed that COs, officers and other ranks remaining in the General Headquarters were ensured permanency of tenure, and physical and moral protection. Major Cayoja, for his part, declared that the COs and officers who are in the military complex remain firmly determined to defend the General Headquarters against any attempt to attack or pillage the establishment. Other officers declared: we do not want a repetition of what happened in 1952. He also stated that among all the officers taking part in this movement [i.e. the fascist coup] the ideas of the institution publicly expressed in the manifesto which they put out last Sunday would continue in force, and be held with the utmost conviction ... 'There are neither victors nor vanquished,' they said, since all of us want a firm basis of unity for the Armed Forces. All problems must be overcome in the most generous spirit of comradeship. They declared that the movement had been fully supported by the establishment, and that they felt their position to have been misinterpreted. They said that General J. J. Torres had agreed to work for the betterment of the Armed Forces, and, they added, 'we believe that he will do so'.

There you have it. It is in fact extremely likely that General Torres will do what they want, and that they will all once again be excellent friends, and overcome all their differences.

Q. Do you believe that the 'Political Command of Workers and People' now being formed stands a chance of making any difference to the result of the crisis?
A. It is hard to form any worth-while opinion about this from here. I have very little information as to what has really happened; the official press, which is all I am allowed to read, is like so many icebergs – only the tip of the news is visible. Furthermore, there have certainly been some imponderable factors, unforeseeable changes and in brief a whole complex situation which it would be hard for any political leadership to handle. In this popular *Comando* there are certain outstanding figures who have proved their worth and their staying power many times at a high political level; but it is clear too that this improvised leadership body at present lacks homogeneity, because it is a simple coalition of different parties or groups, and therefore equally lacks power to make the kind of bold and speedy decisions that are needed in a crisis situation.

But this being said, and with all due respect and prudence, I cannot help asking myself two questions. I wonder first whether there was any justification for the enthusiasm which greeted Torres's coming to the Palace on the part of the COB and this *Comando*, for all the talk of 'popular government' and the 'defeat of fascism' (I take these phrases verbatim from the communiqué issued at the end of the general strike), given that quite obviously the active forces of fascism have not suffered the slightest damage but still hold all their basic positions; and whether, this being so, such an attitude does not foster dangerous illusions (how splendid it would be to get rid of fascism in twenty-four hours by a simple change of president – in the twinkling of an eye!), de-mobilizing the people far too soon, letting it be thought that everything had been achieved by the effect and miracle of some 'secret agreement', and, with no guarantees, no conditions, no changes, dismantling that formidable weapon represented by a general and indefinite strike. I wonder, secondly, whether the following day, when people tried to rectify the mistake they had made the previous day (starting to talk of the 'partial defeat of fascism' – and even that was still somewhat optimistic), they were not perhaps making an error in the opposite direction, an exaggeration as great as the previous one but similar in kind. Having gone forward ten paces, they then went back twenty, renouncing membership of the cabinet for fear of worrying the leaders of the coup in La Paz. Certainly the ideological theory of 'co-government', opportunist and petty bourgeois as it was and sacrificing the class-independence of the proletariat in exchange for a few unimportant cabinet jobs, has been rightly criticized and condemned by the last COB Congress. But as things are at present, at the political rather than the ideological level, to withdraw all demand for cabinet representation amounts to handing over completely to the fascist wing of the Army, yielding to pressure and blackmail before they have even been used. Thus the fabricators of the coup in the General Headquarters, in the Ingavi regiment, in the Military Academy, though failing to reach their optimal objective – i.e. a personal take-over of power – have succeeded in their lesser plan – preventing the people from taking any part in the government – without a single shot being fired, simply by means of one communiqué and a few threatening gestures. The question is one which must at least be asked. I believe it would have been in the interest of the people to try to widen the crack which appeared within the Army, and turn it into an irreparable breach, and prevent so easy a reconciliation at the cost of the workers. Why smooth the way to compromise for Torres? Why thus give him the chance or excuse he needed to avoid giving a clear definition of his policy? Why should he and his group not have been faced with the alternative of either taking a stance once and for all with the country and the popular forces, or removing their disguise for good? Why should he not have been left with the responsibility for plainly and simply refusing the demands of the Political Command and the COB? Certainly it would have been risky, but with the increasingly enthusiastic mobilization of the people and the increasing disorganization and demoralization among the enemy forces supporting the coup, I believe the balance of forces would have come down in favour of the popular side, even allowing for its lack of weapons (a lack which people are well able to remedy in circumstances of this kind). Certainly co-government was no solution: but it was up to General Torres himself to get rid of it so as to improve the general political consciousness. Yet I must admit finally that these questions may only be the result of my own lack of information, and those at present leading the COB must have their reasons for having preferred to avoid a clearer 'definition' of the development now taking place.

In any case, it would seem that the one thing that is certain is that, when it comes to serious definitions in Bolivia at present, in the last instance 'power comes from the barrel of a gun'. After peace had returned to the streets, and it was necessary to form a government, it was clear that there were more guns on the Army's side. It was therefore inevitable that the power should remain in their hands. What might perhaps have been prevented was the concealment under a mass of fine words of the fact that it *was* rule by guns. Though for a time military weapons may appear to be firing pretty bunches of flowers, the real power they represent will inevitably come to the fore again soon.

This is the opinion of a simple observer. It would be better to put your question to those in positions of responsibility.

Q. What difference do you see between the Ovando and Torres governments? Have we merely got a return to the *status quo ante*? A. Though the same phase may be repeated, the clock can never be turned back. The present régime, apart from a few small points in Torres's favour, is a continuation of the Ovando régime, or rather of something which cannot in fact continue any longer at the historical stage Bolivia has reached. That is the paradox, and the reason for the intense frailty of the present system, which would seem to have been accepted by both sides as a kind of parenthesis, an in-between stage. Hence though Ovando did have a certain political credibility (not personally, but in his terms of government) among large sectors of the petty bourgeoisie for some months, a week was enough to leave Torres and his government suspended in mid-air, with no illusions on the part of the popular forces, even those 'progressive' sectors such as were represented by Quiroga Santa Cruz, who had begun by believing in the possibility of the Ovando government's being a success. And unfortunately, or perhaps fortunately, the 'Torres team' got drawn not merely along a road already well-known as a dead-end, but a road that became narrower for them as time went on. His basis of support, and ultimately his freedom of action, has always been more restricted than Ovando's. Like Ovando, he can count neither on the organic support of the intelligent and organized popular forces, nor any organic support from the Right, which has been frustrated without being destroyed. But, furthermore, Torres cannot now even in any formal sense appear as the genuine representative of the combined Armed Forces, but only of a part of them, and that part a small one. To the rest he has become something of a ruler on trial who will have to work hard to hold on to his job: he will be unable to take a step without having to negotiate it, and may have to take two steps backwards in order to be forgiven. To carry out even a hundredth part of his initial promises, the wretched man would have to walk on a knife-edge, under the unfriendly scrutiny of the Armed Forces, without having any firm basis of support on the left. Since it is not possible to do that, he will be wiser not to try, but merely rest content with maintaining the *status quo* in so far as he can. And in the end, even though, as can happen here, a government manages to remain stable for a time, filling in gaps here and there, the class conflict will continue in such a way that he is bound to fall, or (and perhaps as well), more probably, end up carrying out the policies dictated by the Right – after the first few essential gestures – as did Ovando.

But the fate of this particular government is not significant.

What matters is that the crisis has made it possible to go much deeper; so much so that now there can be no straightforward return to the *status quo*. This is so, *a*) because the popular forces have given a clear demonstration of their strength, and consequently are now far more self-confident, and *b*) because many groups have become aware that the last obstacle remaining on the road to power is the lack of a united and strong leadership. That leadership has not yet been established, but it is most certainly on the way to being so, for there is no doubt that the leadership crisis evinced by recent events had very unhappy results. In Oruro and the mines, popular organizations have already become strengthened and pretty well entrenched (having succeeded in collecting a fair amount of arms). The revolutionary political Command of this proletarian town has recently given a public demonstration of the fact that in future the popular forces regard two points as being vital to their programme from a political viewpoint: to solve the problem of political leadership, and make it homogeneous, firm and determined, and to give serious consideration to the problem of forming armed organizations among the proletariat.

Of course, the reaction of the other side is naturally one of self-defence and caution: because it came into contact with the general insurrection at a critical moment and foresaw the possibility of its ending, the right wing also took action and surreptitiously worked its way into an entrenched position; it is well aware that its next crisis may well be its last. Señor Siracusa and the CIA are not taking holidays now.

In short, the problem of power is suspended. Its solution has simply, as though by mutual consent, been postponed. And it is that which perhaps at the present moment provides the justification for the half-hearted centrist mixture of which the Torres government is to be composed; both sides accept it as the lesser of two evils in order to avoid a direct confrontation. To recall Gramsci, though in a different sense, it may be said that this mediocre 'Bonapartism' has been as it were spontaneously generated by a situation of 'a balance of catastrophes', in which both sides – popular revolution and counter-revolution, to give them their simplest description – are frightened of an open and direct conflict because they have a confused feeling that they might simply destroy one another. But I must go on to qualify this by saying that the superiority of the revolutionary side is indubitable because the 'balance of catastrophes' as it is at present is catastrophic only in the sense that the confrontation, since its ending cannot be predicted with one hundred per cent certainty, would have represented a 'catastrophic' civil war, short perhaps, but appalling. In this precarious and tense situation, the compromise formula represented by General Torres and his team has only really been accepted 'to prevent the outpouring of rivers of blood' (to quote one politician who played a fairly active role at the time). A conflagration has been avoided, but I don't believe the gunpowder can be got rid of. The present balance is too unstable, too precarious, too explosive to last long. It is certain to have to collapse. Obviously it is not possible to predict when, but I am inclined to think that it will be soon.

And here it is worth mentioning (but only mentioning, because my knowledge of the Bolivian countryside as it is now is very limited) the third party, silent and discreet, standing in the wings of the social scene: the peasants. Will the country people turn to the proletariat or to the bourgeoisie in the person of its political representative, the Army? It will certainly not be the peasants who unleash the final battle: in Bolivia, revolution moves from town to country (or so the experience – all the experiences, successful and otherwise – of Bolivian history has taught us). But, depending upon whether a proportion of the peasants are won over to the side of the revolution or at least neutralized, or whether they continue to be a fighting reserve for the bourgeoisie, as they were in 1962, may well be what tips the scale. It is a very complex subject, involving a great number of factors; on the immediate level of a popular insurrection in the towns, the speed of the outcome would prevent the military reaction from having the time to bring its reserves into action – that is, its peasants, armed and led by regular troops. Here it would be useful to make a class analysis of peasants, not *en bloc*, but by regions (the Altiplano, the valley of Cochabamba, the areas of settlement in the tropics, the east), and by social levels which may be very different from one another, because of the cultural and racial elements involved. It would be rather a long affair for this exchange, especially since I have not got the data for a concrete investigation apart from what I may happen by chance to hear. But without getting on to the subject, what is obvious is the extraordinary similarity between the analysis of the French peasant 'class' made by Marx in the *Eighteenth Brumaire*, and the situation in the Bolivian countryside since the agrarian reform of 1952. We are faced with a mass of peasants owning tiny strips of land (especially in Valle Grande), without any great sense of solidarity, a prey to usurers and money-lenders, without technical help of any kind, so that really they are more of a *non-class*, defined in terms of being different from the other, city-dwelling, classes, rather than by any consciousness or bonds of their own. The ruling class has nothing more to offer them, presenting them with no prospect of improvement, and yet finds it easy to win their support through the network of *caciques* and official union leaders whom it controls, with a view to defending 'the peasants' property' (their pathetic scraps of land) against 'the communists who want to collectivize everything and take away your hard-won gains'. Undoubtedly the situation has changed considerably in the past few years; peasant discontent is growing in the east, in a quite different way from Valle Grande, for there the peasants have no land at all (there there has been no agrarian reform) and want to turn the large landholdings into cooperatives against the will of the local bourgeoisie and its instrument, the Army. Some time ago the Independent Peasants' Centre was formed, despite constant threats, abuse and even personal physical attacks from successive governments. (This Centre had as its legal adviser Quiroga Bonadona, the president of the COB who died in the guerrilla fighting in Teoponte; it belongs to the COB, and took an active part in the last workers' congress.) The settlers, on the other hand, realized the swindle they had been subjected to, in coming to cultivate tropical land with no guarantee of commercial success, without any real technical help and in the most appalling material conditions (the Colonization Plan was worked out by the BID and its North American advisers in order to relieve the tensions on the Altiplano). We may well recall Marx's phrase, also in the *Eighteenth Brumaire*, which still applies to semi-colonial and predominantly peasant countries (numerically predominant, that is to say), in which he stressed the vital need for 'the proletarian revolution to bring into being the (peasant) chorus without which, in any peasant country, its own solo simply becomes a funeral dirge'.

Hence the quiet but bitter 'struggle for the countryside' being fought by the opposing forces of the revolution and the counter-revolution (in which the latter have the great initial advantage of controlling the apparatus of the State, of which the official peasant trade unions are a part). Under the aegis of the COB, a 'Worker–Peasant Pact' was signed when, during the period of the crisis, peasant militia from Cochabamba arrived in El Alto de la Paz to complete the rout of the fascist coup. Yet only a few days later, once the Armed Forces had become aware of the situation, they returned to ratify the 'Military–Peasant Pact' which was actually a series of reciprocal guarantees between officers and the docile peasant *caciques*, but which has already been broken in several provinces.

As for the most suitable ways of working politically in peasant circles, that is another major problem; it has its own special and varying solutions in Bolivia, but this is not the place to study them.

Q. Peru and Bolivia are often linked together. Can these military régimes be measured by the same yardstick? How would you characterize what is happening in Peru?
A. This supposed parallel is a convenient cliché, but there is no basis at all for it in history. Nothing could be more superficial or false. The internal class relations in the two countries are very different. Though economically more backward, Bolivia is far more advanced politically. In Peru, the workers' movement has

been distorted and corrupted by the APRA[1] almost from the first. Peru has nothing like the kind of concentration of workers that we have with the miners here. It has no one workers' centre with that kind of tradition of struggle, or political maturity. Above all, Peru has never had the experience of a popular revolution such as Bolivia had in 1952, despite its ultimate failure because of its reformist leadership: for the Peruvian masses, even reformism is something new – whereas for the Bolivians it is already out of date. In Peru, finally, and perhaps above all, there was no Che to fight to the death. In short, the class struggle in Bolivia has objectively reached a higher stage, which objectively demands a better political definition than a merely progressive government. In other words, the history of the Bolivian nation shows that it is time for the proletariat to take over the reins of power, that this is the moment for the construction of socialism. The proof of this lies in front of us, even though it be negative. A 'revolution' in the petty bourgeois style, without a clearly socialist sense, is simply impossible in Bolivia now, because there can be no revolutionary dynamic without a mobilization of the masses, and the masses will no longer be mobilized by a reformist programme, nor are they prepared to follow a 'centrist' régime. Hence the congenital failure of both the Ovando and the Torres régimes. It may be that Velasco Alvarado, after two years in power, can draw masses to the Plaza San Martín, but it is quite certain that Torres today could not lead a popular movement in La Paz. Indeed, he is condemned to be afraid of the people, because if the people should be mobilized they would not rally to Torres but to their own leaders, and their own class aims. If it comes to the crunch, they will leave the petty bourgeois, and their terminology and their ideological inconsistency and their ineffective sell-outs, and immediately plant the seeds of revolution as put forward in the programme of the FSTMB (Federación Sindical de los Trabajadores Mineros de Bolivia)[2] and the thesis of the COB.

Many observers have noted, and many foreign journalists and

1. American Popular Revolutionary Alliance.
2. The Miners' Trade Union.

tourists have been surprised by, the considerable difference in style between the political behaviour of the Peruvian officers and that of the 'progressive' officers in Bolivia. The former, sure of themselves and untroubled, are capable of repeated daring political moves, without fear or hesitation, as though step by step carrying out a strategic plan. The latter, nervous, confused, hesitant, self-contradictory, lacking any long-term plans or real homogeneity, follow a policy of changes and delays, of passivity and temporizing, looking no further than a week ahead – a policy not of preparing for danger, but of dealing arbitrarily with threats and risks individually only as they present themselves. This difference is not due to any lack of personal ability, nor to any psychological or cultural factors. It represents a different stage in history. The Peruvian officers do what they do well, because they have to do it, because they are filling in a historical gap, carrying out an objective role – the role of involving Peruvian society in a movement that is bourgeois–democratic, just beginning, genuine, thrusting forward – a role which the 'progressive' bourgeois class has fulfilled in other times and other countries. The Bolivian 'progressive' officers are doing what little they do badly, because fundamentally all this has already been done, in so far as bourgeois–democratic tendencies can do it, and what remains to be done is to build up revolutionary socialism, a task which must be performed by others than the uniformed petty bourgeoisie. The situation of Bolivian reformism is a sad one: some reforms have already been made, but now those that remain to be made can only be made by a socialist revolution led by the proletariat. Sad too is the situation of those who seek to play the role of populist leaders: they cannot yet lead any popular movement without betraying it in the short term, and if they want to share in, or be part of a popular movement, then they must give up the idea of leading it.

The programme, the tasks, the confused ideology (confused because it combines, under the nationalist banner, both popular nationalism and bourgeois nationalism), the multi-class organization of the political front (or rather, its lack of organization, which is a concrete reflection of its lack of theoretical definition), all these correspond to the period of the MNR, the national revolution of 1952, and have no content. The tree, having given its fruit in season, has now dried up. Attempts to bring it back to life without injecting it with a new programme, a new idea, a new ideology in tune with the present historical situation, are condemned to failure. Latin America is no longer living in the period of Cárdenas but of Fidel Castro (not as regards *methods* of action, but as regards the *content* of any possible action). This has been recognized by the most honest, clear-sighted, and genuine factions of the old revolutionary nationalism. They now realize that the task is a socialist one, and that the leadership must come from the proletariat; they are abandoning the centrist childishness which caused their failure before, and refuse to have any part in the solutions – and irresolutions! – of the petty bourgeois authorities of the day, because they know them to be condemned to fail, and that knowledge they have from their own experience. This evolution, or this growth to political adulthood, intelligently accepted by some of those most active in the last revolution, reflects something which seems to me even more important and encouraging: the radicalization of large bodies of the middle class, who have grasped that capitalism, as it works out in a semi-colonial country, can offer them nothing, can do nothing to ameliorate their lives, but will only produce a continuous, rapidly worsening underdevelopment. A splendid example of this tendency is the position taken up by the National Confederation of Professionals, made up of doctors, lawyers, engineers, architects, teachers, etc., who, far from attacking the present government from right-wing positions, attack it from the left, and have made it absolutely clear that the professional class is ready not to lead, but to enrol as junior members in a popular régime, under the leadership of the national proletariat and supporting socialist aims.

Everything looks as though the special balance of forces in Bolivia would be one of opposition between a sub-bourgeoisie and a sub-proletariat. Therefore the groups in between find themselves attracted towards the pole which their informed historical intuition tells them to be the decisive one. This is a determining element in the formation of a popular revolutionary bloc, that under the leadership of the factory and mining proletariat there will also gather the poor peasants and the petty bourgeoisie (professionals, intellectuals and students).

Any régime lacking the support of such a bloc or, rather, any régime that tries to elude the basic dilemmas between socialism and capitalism, the proletariat and the bourgeoisie, under the guise of some kind of Third Term (Third World, neither with the one nor the other, 'not so much an enemy to the rich, as a friend to the poor', etc.), can never be described as 'progressive'. That does not mean that a popular government would solve all problems in a day; nor that the construction of socialism in Bolivia will be easy. It does mean that only a radical and popular régime, rooted in the working class, can fulfil a historically progressive function in Bolivia. The class basis is what matters – not the manner of government, which need not be specially radical in style, as long as the rhythm of socialist development, the target of its attack, and the choice of its allies, all basically follow from circumstances as they actually are. What is indisputable is the basis of social support, for that is the one and only guarantee for the future.

IV Correspondence with Chato Peredo

At the end of December 1969, the ELN, deeply affected by the death of Inti Peredo and subject to relatively effective repression, proceeded to carry out a somewhat ambitious programme of expropriation, starting with an attack on a bank in La Paz which seems to have ended in semi-failure: the 'recent events in La Paz' alluded to in the beginning of the first letter published here refer to that.

These letters were not signed, and no names are mentioned, for obvious reasons. However, Chato Peredo's answer was published in Chile while he himself was on the way to Teoponte, whereas, for technical reasons, my letters were not. Though not connected with the problems under discussion, and oddly formal in style, I have added the handwritten message sent to me by Chato in Chile, where we both were after being set free, as a kind of symbolic and provisional conclusion.

1 Letter from Régis Debray to the ELN of Bolivia

Slow and Sure is better than Hasty and Unsuccessful
(re an inopportune statement)

Many comrades have been justifiably concerned by a declaration made on my behalf by my French lawyer saying that 'I disapproved of recent events in La Paz'. And it is true that I do disapprove of them; but this is something I must explain in political terms, and not in the kind of personal context which would seem to be suggested in this cable. It is not wise here to compromise with anyone, still less so when they have recently talked of amnesty in such frequently ambiguous terms as 'mercy', 'pardon', 'generosity', etc. – outrageous terms which we cannot for a moment accept. But

I will leave this perspective, or rather lack of perspective, aside for the present, and go on to analyse the situation.

Earlier on I reminded the comrades that in Camiri we get no news of anything or anyone until long after things have happened (which is why I have only just found out what really happened in La Paz, or rather what the bourgeois press *says* happened). My political isolation is little short of total because of the impossibility of discussing these matters with any comrades, since there are none in Camiri; and in this darkness I have to find what light I can by whatever means are available – which are almost nil – to try to see anything at all.

The day after the *Día de la Dignidad*, just after the nationalization of Gulf Oil, I wrote some notes about the present petty bourgeois government, and both the good and the bad elements of the reformist process taking place, at least as it was then. I shall not repeat them, partly for lack of time, and partly because in three months it is likely that more may have come to be known. The foreseeable move to the right would seem to have begun in mid-December, but the precise date makes no difference to the basis of the analysis, confirming both the class nature of the present government, and the twofold system of contradictions which force it by turns into opposition to Yankee imperialism and to the informed labouring masses. Having done something to injure the former, it was necessary to set up some barrier to the pressing demand of the latter; if it did not do that the government would lose control of proceedings and simply have to withdraw from revolution properly so called, or at least from any clear popular position. This government knows intuitively that it lacks any real capacity for political and ideological leadership, so much so that it foresees that any such leadership would be bound to slip out of its hands should the masses and their trade union and political vanguards really come to the fore. In addition there is the far greater position of weakness in which the 'progressive' wing stands today (i.e. most of the civilians) because of the economic problems arising from nationalization. It was that wing which pushed through almost all the positive measures adopted up to now, thus using up its reserves of influence and power. The initiative now lies with self-confessed reactionaries, who are moving into a general counter-attack. It is noteworthy that this kind of pendulum movement may still have some surprises in store, and it is quite possible that there will be another swing to the left later on.

Nevertheless, we must not play into the hands of the right wing by allowing them to talk of 'an anti-national left-wing conspiracy' and so on. Things are not yet far enough advanced. The people have to become thoroughly convinced *by experience* of the illusory nature of reformism, of the fact that the state apparatus has not basically changed, that the *gorilas* still hold the key posts, that the mechanism of repression remains intact, and so on. We cannot and must not harbour illusions about 'a national pattern of development', which simply means a semi-state capitalism in the hands of the commercial and bureaucratic bourgeoisie. But these illusions must be destroyed by events, and it must be the class struggle moving forward irresistibly and spontaneously that destroys them. As yet the contradictions have not become evident. They have begun to be glimpsed first in the failure to raise the wages of the miners, secondly in the statement (which would be funny if it were not so sinister) that there are no political prisoners in the country, and that there is therefore no legal basis for an amnesty. Let me make this clear: it is certainly not a question of having an anti-everything policy, or systematically opposing everything the government does, nor of course of letting oneself be defeated by imperialist propaganda. That would be as immoral as it is stupid. On the contrary, the government is *even now* caught in a dilemma, between the people and the national capitalist oligarchy, between the left and the right, between the 'defence of western civilization' (Torres) and the recognition of the historical justification for revolutionary socialism – especially that of Cuba, even though it may not share it (Ortiz, Quiroga, etc.); therefore it is up to us to do everything we can to force it on to the democratic path, to wrest economic and social victories from it, to reorganize the workers' movement, and to carry all these actions as far as we can. So much so that it will be the régime itself which will be forced to state its position in relation to the people's demands, and to make clear whose side it is on. Of course, as Marxists, we already know what changes must occur if laws are to be passed which really allow for historical development. But our theoretical knowledge must be converted into practical experience for the majority of the people, and that too is an objective process which cannot be artificially hurried on without risking a loss of contact with most of the popular forces – for they may well not yet understand attitudes of open belligerency until tomorrow or the next day; indeed they will only understand them when they themselves come to demand them.

We struggle not for the sake of struggling, but in order to win. The armed struggle is not an end in itself, but like war, according to Lenin and Clausewitz, it is simply the continuation of politics by other means. The political direction of that struggle is therefore the basis and the determining factor of a correct political line, which is itself based on a true appreciation of the conditions in force *at a given moment*. There can be no decisions, feelings, moral commitments in the abstract, without taking account of the concrete possibilities; and what is right today may be, and undoubtedly will be, wrong tomorrow. In politics as in life, there is a rhythm: there are times for preparing to act and times for acting, times for gathering one's forces and times for using them, times for identifying with the masses, and times for taking a step ahead of them (not ten steps at once though). I believe that at present we are in the first kind of period.

If we struggle in order to win, and if winning is not possible at any and every moment, how are we to determine the right moment? A time of general crisis – and I need not repeat here the three Leninist criteria for defining a crisis situation. 'Those on top' have still not revealed their internal oppositions, 'those below' have seen how to become open to any prospect of emancipation – however partial, obscure, indeterminate – that may present itself. But this has only happened recently: it was not true six months ago, when the mines were concentration camps, when everything was subject to the laws of State security, when there was total and undisputed subservience to imperialism. There may still be illusions or false hopes, and we must see what time will bring. A year from now the situation will be clearer; either we shall be able to look forward to a really democratic and anti-imperialist development (which is unlikely), or (more likely) the bourgeois and the *gorilas* will have disposed of that once and for all. As things are now, if the ELN were to move into an open position of attack, it would be supremely isolated, and more exposed than ever to nationalist–bourgeois propaganda. The time that has elapsed since September has still not been enough to enable the working class to be reorganized. A large proportion of the urban middle classes have been confused by the officers' speeches, and feel that they are best represented in the government by the civilian ministers. It is doubtful whether there could be any serious work of political implantation in the countryside. In these conditions, the bourgeois apparatus of repression has complete freedom and capacity for action, and the balance of forces is against us in a way it has never been in the past and will certainly never again be in the future. The problem is to know whether we want to go on making martyrs of those who might become effective and victorious fighters in the future, or whether we really want our sacrifices to have some purpose, to be of some use to the people.

To suit the situation as it is *now*, it would be better for the organization to work towards achieving a serious and definite change in the political situation, though it is impossible to say whether it will come about sooner or later.

Internal recruitment and organization must be improved, with the object first and foremost of greater efficiency and the achievement of strength and fitness for greater tasks. That means that security must be drastically improved before anything important can be undertaken. There has been quite obvious infiltration, with the enemy working against the organization night and day, both before the 'revolutionary' coup and since. What is the use of exposing comrades to the risk of death without having provided the best possible conditions for protecting them? Perhaps there are too many cadres? Perhaps there is so much money and so many provisions that we can't help making the police a present of some of it every three months?

To increase internal security is not only a problem of techniques, of working in small groups, of discipline. At bottom it is a problem which must be resolved by means of raising the level of people's political awareness through internal political work. Experience (of which I have had plenty) teaches that it is more dangerous to give someone (because he appears to be in sympathy with the cause) technical or military training without having first considered his political training – without, that is, discovering his convictions and his capacity for holding to them in times of stress. Anyone, a police officer or a petty bourgeois, can learn to handle explosives; what not everyone can do is to have the humility and patience to study the whole ideology, and then place what he has learnt at the service of the people. To ask an infiltrator to capture an American-made gun presents no problem. But ask him why he actually wants to create a revolution, and after one or two clichés he has learnt he will have nothing more to say.

We have to gather our forces and unite with the masses – in other words, enter fully into all their material and economic problems; work in the unions, raise the level of consciousness, absorb the atmosphere, learn to recognize which men we can count upon and which not, and so on. We must continue to train cadres, and become cadres ourselves. I cannot go into greater detail here, but what is chiefly needed is agility and imagination. Remember that the Tupamaros did not come into being all at once, but that Sendic and his comrades worked for years secretly mixing with the sugar-workers in the north and then with people in the cities; that they paid enormous attention to security and to the political training of their members; that they waited to act until the oligarchy in Uruguay collapsed in chaos, until it became clear that the government had absolutely no sense of social, economic or political purpose; that they then judged their action by political criteria, directing it to carefully chosen objects, making clear each time that it was part of the struggle of the masses, and linking up everything they did with the trade union and political struggles of the time; that they practised what might be called 'terrorism by the masses' in the sense that in most cases they acted in concert with and in defence of the workers' interests and their economic demands, kidnapping employers or others responsible for laying workers off or lowering wages, giving money publicly to workers' organizations by getting ransoms paid, etc.; that they attacked objectives known by all to be anti-popular and oligarchic, like luxury casinos, large importing firms, members of the rich oligarchy, and so on; and that all that developed logically into what might be called 'a public clandestinity', explaining the purpose of every armed action in leaflets, radio programmes, and even announcing them beforehand to the public at large, working through the press and public opinion to avoid the danger of cutting themselves off from the masses.

We can leave bourgeois reformism here to be bogged down by its own weight without allowing it any good excuse for its failure, and certainly without letting it lay the blame on the revolutionary left. The militarist right which still stands by the State apparatus, the bourgeois power which remains intact in the factories, the newspapers, the town councils outside the capital, the presence of imperialism and its allies within the Army and the ministries, the whole machinery of 'aid' – all these must first be unmasked and shown for what they are doing, and what they are, this to be achieved through open, legal and combative action by the masses, until the majority of the people are clearly aware that all these people must be fought, in the city streets and in the mountains.

I hope that the comrades will talk over these problems, and let me know what they have to add to or delete from what I have said, whether they agree or not. This work of determining a correct line must be seen as a collective and ever-changing task.

The author will be delighted by any revolutionary criticism you have to offer.

Camiri, 1970

2 Reply from Chato Peredo

A battle may be won or lost, but it must be fought . . .

Che

Though it is somewhat late, we are replying to your helpful elucidation of certain statements attributed to you some time ago in the press. The passage of time has cast light on several points in your letter. Some of your suggestions are extremely wise and accurate, and we take considerable note of them as coming from a revolutionary. However, it is necessary to highlight other aspects which may look rather different to those actually within the situation, and still others which have simply been forgotten.

Superficially, and in the view of a lot of revolutionaries, our attitude (and the events of the end of last year to which you refer) could appear to represent desperation or 'deviationism' in the dual political situation in which the people are (as always) in conflict with the forces of reaction. There is an 'arbitrator' in the middle: he will yield to one side or the other depending on the pressures, but ultimately he represents the interests of the one of which he is an active member, and he allows himself the luxury of playing the 'democratic game' only so long as there is no threat to the stability of the system he supports.

The right needs no excuse to talk about 'anti-national left-wing conspiracies'. It is not a matter of dealing with the storm by analysing a piece of Bolivian history (insignificant in both time and space), or that of any other country in this continent. Our life as a republic (compared pictorially with the swing of a pendulum) can be summed up thus:

From the colonialist reaction (on the right) there rose the independentist revolution (which for convenience we may call left). That was followed by the establishment of Creole feudalism (right), up to the period of European-born liberalism (left – at least for domestic consumption at the time). Then came the reinforcing of the mining 'super-state' accompanied by Yankee penetration (right) which came up against the obstacles of Busch and Villaroel (left) until it became firmly entrenched with later governments (right).

1952, within the framework of the capitalist structure, produced a qualitative change which opened broad social possibilities, but the movement lacked a vanguard to develop those aspirations or direct it towards the proper goals. This predicament of the left led inevitably into the reactionary dictatorship of Barrientos (right) but, to keep the pendulum swinging, there then came the populism of Ovando (left). Right, left, right, left . . . but in each 'new' situation, despite certain nuances and characteristics which delude many people, the basic structure has remained unchanged.

Well then, what is our role in this endless swinging back and forth? Are we to be carried back and forth with it? Are we to wait for developments to occur spontaneously?

Certainly politics, like life, has its own rhythm; its times of preparation and times of action. But there was a time when biological development made a *spontaneous* social development possible – so much so that man is now capable of actually *directing* biological changes, to say nothing of social ones. Obviously it is hard to regulate the speed of any process at will, but man's role is to do what he can by smoothing the road at some times, and placing obstacles along it at others. The combination of mutations was the origin of new species. But socially things are rather different. Thus, in our process, the period of preparation does not exclude action, since action may also play a part in speeding up the necessary preparation for the decisive struggle.

There is a tendency on the part of fringe groups, of some of our supporters, to belittle our political analysis, and label us as merely 'ditherers'. Others consider that we are too much committed to the past and to our own dead. And it is true, we have got moral and political commitments to those who came before us, who fought for the final liberation of Bolivia and all South America. We are totally committed to Bolívar, Sucre, Che, Inti, etc., and no vagueness or confusion in our situation will ever lead us to abandon that commitment.

But please understand that that commitment is not the same as an obsession with tactical action; it will remain in force as long as our American homeland has not been freed once and for all.

Whoever may compose the vanguard who finally win that struggle, we shall be satisfied to have contributed something towards it.

We are not attaching ourselves to the government's 'wagon' as long as it has no clear and definite direction, as long as it produces endless circumlocutions and is involved in foolish self-contradictions into which it is led by its fear of the forces of reaction (which clearly control the real power). Such involvement is a game of cat and mouse in which the official 'Left', satisfied by the few positive measures it has taken, believes itself to be playing the part of the cat, but always end up as the mouse.

It must be recognized that the ultra-reactionaries are worried and are continually planning a coup; and the government will make the most of that fact to touch the heart-strings of the people. But recent popular demonstrations have given an indication of just what the people's feelings are – and they are not, as the government used to think, entirely in its favour.

The last Miners' Congress, the student demonstrations, etc., were indicative, and in any case it has been impossible to ignore what the guerrillas are doing. The government has used up all its so-called revolutionary chances, at least in the economic sphere. They still have a few purely political cards left to play, such as granting amnesty to our prisoners. We shall not be against this. But our attitude is not to support what little may be done, but constantly to condemn what is not done – which often passes unnoticed, whereas what *is* done is blown up out of all proportion, precisely as a cover-up for what is not being done.

We do not believe the government's own definition of itself. It is circumstances which define every process, and no *gorila*, however much he may believe in ultimate victory, is going to try to enforce a cruel and repressive dictatorship as long as events are not favourable. Consider what happened in Uruguay, the 'Switzerland of Latin America' to refer again to the example of the Tupamaros, while the traditional parties of the left (Arismendi among others) talked of 'gathering their forces', the first shots rang out, alarming and surprising national – and international – opinion. Did the authorities then think in terms of a repression?

There was no need, no reason to do so. It was a 'developing' but undefined process. Then trade unionist and institutionalist methods were suitable, and indeed necessary in order to move on to a higher stage in the struggle – the armed struggle, which is the only struggle that is truly and effectively liberating. And the armed struggle in Uruguay did not begin from a position of support by the masses (the mass parties in fact condemned such methods). To give a still vividly recent example, we may quote Chile, with a situation similar to that of Uruguay, where repression has already been unleashed against revolutionary groups.

'We struggle to conquer; we cannot conquer at every moment, and how are we to decide which moment is right? There are times of crisis . . .' Such crisis moments do not always occur, and at present no such situation exists. We are not simply waiting for the 'opportune moment', but are trying to bring it about, trying to impose clear definition upon a government which will not define itself as long as no one else defines it.

The phrase of Lenin and Clausewitz, that 'war is no more than the continuation of politics by other means', must be put the other way round for most of our countries: the continuation of politics by other means is nothing more than war.

This war is a long-term affair, and is a preparation for the moment of revolutionary crisis when the slightest move will show up the instability of the system; meanwhile the efforts will be enormous, and will cost us brave lives, not in any 'pointless waste' of cadres, but because the needs of the struggle demand it.

'Exposing comrades to the risk of death without having provided the *best possible* conditions for protecting them?' (the italics are mine). Let me ask you: what does it mean to provide the best possible conditions of protection? Every action of ours is a politico-military action. If we expropriate a bank, we are carrying out a political-cum-military operation, and not an ordinary gangster's attack. Therefore it is superfluous to talk of what means of security are to be taken; we know that in every action there are risks, that the unforeseeable may always arise at any moment, and that things will never always go according to plan. In fact, however many conditions we may provide for any kind of action, with whatever purpose it is undertaken, they can never ensure a hundred per cent guarantee of success. To create the 'best possible conditions' would mean to have a perfect infrastructure upon which to base the revolution, and this has for many years been a matter of deepest concern to the leaders of the 'revolutionary parties'. The policy of creating the *best possible conditions* inevitably leads to making success one's sole criterion, and thinking of partial failures in an abstract and remote way – so that when they occur there is greater demoralization among those for whom success is all that matters.

The harshness, length and difficulty of our struggle is rooted not only in physical sacrifice, but in the political, military and even ideological setbacks we come up against.

The process has its ups and downs. We shall undergo moments as difficult as, or even more difficult than, those following the death of Che, but as long as we can be sure that our struggle *continues,* we can be certain that it will finally triumph. We have no opportunity for political manoeuvre. 'A step back in order to be able to take two steps forward' in these circumstances, would mean remaining where we had stepped back, and having to step back still further.

The enemy keeps reinforcing their methods of repression, and only by using counter-methods of our own can we form ourselves into a fighting force that will finally become invincible. It is essential that we have an ideology, a policy, a mystique, and so on; these are essential, but they are not enough to bring us victory.

I would like to conclude by copying out a paragraph from Che's *Guerrilla Warfare: a Method.* You can draw your own conclusions:

... Marx always recommended that once the revolutionary movement had begun the proletariat must strike and strike again. A revolution that does not continue to grow deeper is a revolution that is retreating. Those who are fighting tire, begin to lose faith and may then try to profit from some of the manoeuvres with which the bourgeoisie have made us so familiar. These might be elections, resulting in the coming to power of another gentleman with an even pleasanter voice and more angelic face than the outgoing dictator, or a coup by reactionaries, *generally led by the army, and supported, directly or indirectly, by progressive forces* [italics mine]. There are others, but it is not my purpose to analyse tactical stratagems.

Let us draw attention principally to the manoeuvre of the military coup imposed from above. What have officers got to contribute to any genuine democracy? . . .

When, in situations that are difficult for the oppressors, the military conspire and overthrow a dictator, their having defeated him leads one to suppose that they did it because he could no longer preserve their class privileges without intense violence, which is something that does not generally at present suit the interests of the oligarchies . . .

Let us repeat once again our gratitude to and affection for you as a comrade in the struggle, and a member of the army founded by Che. Your views, however different they may be from ours, do nothing to diminish your stature as a revolutionary in our eyes.

With a revolutionary embrace, and in hope of a reply, I send my greetings.

VICTORY OR DEATH!

BACK TO THE MOUNTAINS!

3 Reply to Chato Peredo from Régis Debray

I was delighted to get a letter from you. As you say, the passage of time does help to make everything clearer, and it is precisely this factor of time, this essential and fundamental factor in all political activity, which makes the interchange of opinions between us somewhat pointless as regards any *practical* outcome. We are obviously in agreement over fundamentals, over strategy, objectives and the will to achieve them. What concerns me is how to work the strategy into the situation, how to make the most of every opportunity, how to bring our ship safely into port. Remember Lenin and his about-turns, his sudden changes, his tactical

– and incredibly disconcerting – flexibility between, say, April and October 1917. This strikes me specially because Kerensky's government was at bottom as counter-revolutionary as Ovando's. But Lenin made the most of those few months to reorganize his workers' party among the masses, to throw into sharp relief the contradictions of the situation, and finally to prepare for open warfare, for a direct attack when the moment came – after the rising of Kornilov and the unmasking of the basic complicity existing between the petty bourgeois government and the militarist reactionaries.

Now, in May 1970, the time, your time, for great actions is also coming. I cannot foresee precisely when, but anyone can see that it is imminent. The growing movement of the masses ever since January, their increased consciousness, their reorganization (miners, workers, students, and sections of the middle class such as journalists) has been such that this government, congenitally incapable of ruling, will once again have to have recourse to force; it must set up a dam, if it is not to be swept away by the flood. That is quite certain. But these seven or eight months of semi-freedom, of semi-tolerance, have undoubtedly been of use to the people. Surely, if you are going into battle, and the enemy, whether through carelessness, internal disputes, or because he cannot do otherwise, gives you a short time to dig your trenches, clean your guns, prepare your lines of retreat and your logistical bases, improve your knowledge of the terrain, and even to rest and re-coup your strength – surely that time is most welcome? That was all I meant to say.

As for assessing the situation, that is a sheer impossibility in the material conditions in which I am placed. Imagine: I have one contact with the external world every four months when my wife and my lawyer visit me! If I write something today, when it is finally published it will be irrelevant – I refer to tactical writings, since other kinds have no special urgency nor perhaps usefulness either. Thus, two days after the nationalization of Gulf Oil, I wrote some quick notes on the situation, which might have had some validity for a month or so, after which I would no longer have agreed with them myself, because the situation had simply changed; and when they were finally published four months later in Cuba they were no more than a joke. I mention this unimportant incident only to give you an example of the kind of limitations I refer to. Add to this the lack of information (my one source is *Presencia*, that piece of pre-conciliar trash – pre the Council of Trent I mean – which would have been up-to-date in 1500), solitude, the inability to have any interchange of revolutionary opinions with anyone here, and you will understand why I find it difficult to say anything intelligent about 'what is going on'. However, let me add in parenthesis that I have the greatest interest when someone is moved to La Paz, or the Panóptico, or anywhere else, though my interest would be even greater if it were myself whom they were transferring to some other part of the world!

To give a broad outline of what has happened up to now, and so that you may know my general position, let me sum up thus: from October until the beginning of February, there was a national–bourgeois government, whose intentions were of some interest and usefulness, and which showed possibilities, though they were few and remote, that it might be converted in spite of itself by mass action, 'critical support', pressure from below and a little manipulation from above, into a national–popular government – provided a genuine civilian-cum-military bloc could be formed, and the most fiercely right-wing political group in the Army be isolated and got rid of, etc. (All this of course while continuing to go forward on both feet – the legal and illegal, with less stress on the latter.) In February, the government capitulated to the Congress of 'national' capitalists[1] and the Conclave of Miraflores,[2] where

1. The *Congreso de los capitalistas nacionales*: this refers to a Congress of Free Enterprise which, disturbed by the steps towards nationalization taken by the government, forced Ovando to give Bolivian employers a number of guarantees, among others that he would never decide to socialize the means of production.

2. The *Conclave de Miraflores*: Miraflores is the central Army Headquarters in La Paz. There, in February 1970, all unit commanders met, and interviewed the ministers of the government, especially the 'progressive' civilian

the Army, under the pretext of a united establishment, once again took control of what was going on. The fundamental hesitancy of the petty bourgeoisie throughout history appeared here in one of its most grotesque and typical forms. The Marx of the *Eighteenth Brumaire* or *The Civil War in France* would have enjoyed the smoothness of it all, though the spectacle, despite its theoretical – almost canonical – perfection, was sad indeed. From March until 15 May – i.e. today, this sorcerer's apprentice of a régime has been burning its hands in the water which it has itself boiled in order to live up to its liberal reputation as a conciliator above and outside all classes. In other words, it cannot stop the meetings of miners or journalists or the COB Congresses; it cannot stop the student revolution; it cannot submit to having its disguise removed and having an end put to all the illusions. But it is frightened by the level of awareness of the masses, their spirit of independence and their class consciousness, their intelligent support of socialism and their tremendous power. Consequently, it is moving sharply backwards, and the familiar faces of the *gorilas* are once again appearing (or, if you prefer, the true face of the *gorila* can now be seen); the basic structure of Barrientos is being re-established on the same socio-political base, that is the manipulation of the peasants by means of 'Agreements' between them and the Army. The workers' ideal, though two months earlier it was still 're-spected and accepted' as a free opinion of free citizens in a free bourgeois Republic is now rejected, and once again the time has come for an 'anti-subversive' campaign, in other words, really a campaign against what we call revolution but they call subversion. The petty bourgeoisie are chewing their nails on finding that they cannot play either with the masses or with the word 'revolution', for the simple reason that they have no hegemonic power of any kind over the revolutionary movement of the masses. They now find themselves faced with the dilemma of either follow-ing the 'revolutionary' and 'anti-imperialist' road (as they under-

---

ministers, to make them give an account of their stewardship, and explain some of their more 'regrettable' declarations – i.e. those of a democratic or liberal turn.

stand it) and giving up all idea of directing matters, or, on the other hand, of keeping the leadership in their own military hands, but leaving the road they were on before. For the two are irreconcilable. I do not believe that these people are sufficiently self-sacrificing to give up their positions of command; I do not believe the Army will hand over its weapons to the workers on a silver plate. So, if what I have said up to now still means anything, then we are entering upon the second path of overt counter-revolution.

This is a broad outline without any definite dates or places. It seems to me that events from now on will be precipitated. But I don't conceal the fact that, in my perhaps mistaken or mis-informed view, it would be to the advantage of the popular forces not to respond to the provocations of the repressive forces. It is better to leave it to the government itself to engage in open warfare. Its destruction must be total and the *evident* result of its own behaviour, under the simple, continuing, and overt attacks of the people fighting for their rights and interests. Don't worry. I do not believe it will last long. It is a matter of a few months, perhaps only weeks, as far as I can see. It is not possible yet to say or to convince anyone that the police raid on the university campus a few days ago was a mistake. But when they have done it two or three times, in one form or another, then the 'mistakes' will have become something the whole world sees as a policy, and then a requiem mass for Barrientos will no longer be merely a formality. And I am convinced that if by some miracle this government as it is now behaving, wavering, cautious, and careful in its use of re-pression, should last another two or three months, those months might perhaps be no bad thing for the popular organizations, including our own. You would know this better than I; but it would provide a chance to become stronger, to prepare for the confron-tation from all points of view – material, political, economic, etc. For the problem is the problem of the future. What are we going to put in the place of what is there now? Another fourth of November, another Barrientos, another Miranda, after another little MNR-like development? Or will there this time be a real revolution rather than the traditional military *coup d'état*? That is what matters – that the pendulum, as you say, should not swing back to where it was before, in that traditional movement you describe so well, and which sums up Bolivian history, moving between an ambiguous populism and a frank and unambiguous reaction. What matters to us is that the ambiguous populism of the past which today seems to be in its death-throes should be followed not by the usual overt and clearly-defined counter-revolution, but by a genuinely revolutionary régime. Very well then. What does it take to make a revolution? A struggle, and essentially an armed struggle. And what makes the struggle successful? Organization. That is not something which can be set up in three days. It is the result of much hard work on all sides, and I see no harm at all in their allowing us a slightly longer time to work. You must of course forgive my talking of 'us' – not so much because I am a foreigner, but because I am a prisoner, and from where I am it is not possible to work at all in that sense. I am in relative comfort, and must be patient – though my patience is nearing an end – and above all, I am intolerably powerless to act. I realize that pieces of advice from someone quite so isolated, inactive and lacking in any responsibility may well fall upon you as so many strange and purposeless meteorites. All I can offer is an opinion, and I only regret that it must be that of a mere spectator, from somewhere up in the clouds (not that there are many clouds in my five-metres-square yard!).

What about the amnesty? I do not share your view that this government may still play that particular card. It cannot, for the Army will never allow it. The rumours to that effect are the sheerest deceptions, ways of temporizing, of soothing people's demands, a method of gaining time, of uttering vague noises to conceal the government's total inability to issue any such decree. I can no longer have any illusions on the subject, though, for obvious reasons, it is in the government's best interests to keep me deluded. They are afraid of problems. The easiest way to prevent problems is to keep talking. I thought of putting out a statement which, as far as I am concerned, would have put an end to all the deceptions, to this game of receiving demands, studying the demands, satisfying the people who have made the demands, and so forth. It seems to me that none of this gets us any further, but may even have the reverse effect by making people believe in the possibility of some solution coming from above, and thus preventing their seeking the only effective ways to a solution, which must come from below. But I must put that off due to an unexpected interruption. I wanted at least to let you know my point of view in the matter. The time for an amnesty is past, precisely because the time for fighting is coming. Then the question of prisoners will no doubt be resolved by the same active means as in other neighbouring countries – where there exists a strong enough organization to make such action free of excessive risks. But I suppose that, when the time comes, there will be discussion through other means. For the moment, let us say two months, the unrest of the masses is fulfilling a useful role.

For your note is very clear that this government must be recognized not only for what little it *is* doing, but for all that it is *not* doing. There were many measures which might have been expected and have not been taken, and the absence of events in various fields should certainly not remain unnoticed, especially when they try to cover up that absence with a lot of fine words. And I deeply regret that in this matter of the amnesty it has not been possible to put an end once and for all, definitely and publicly, to the double game of publicity which the government is playing by letting rumours or suggestions or promises slip out every two or three months in some little ministerial or presidential statement here and there, while inside, within the military High Command where all the decisions are actually made, there remains an absolute and definite decision against it.

Thank you for your kind words. Though our opinions may differ, I believe that each time they grow closer; we made different assessments of the relation between tactics and strategy, between the short and the long term, between ends and means, but the passage of time alone has been enough to resolve much of the difference. You may guess with what interest I am looking forward to the day when we can meet one another and talk properly, and if need be untangle our misunderstandings. Meanwhile, I assure you that here there is total solidarity and support for all of you.

With the revolutionary greetings of your comrade, R. D.

Camiri (no date).

4 Letter to Régis Debray from Chato Peredo and his Comrades

Comrade Debray,

We are sincerely delighted by the fact of your liberation, which we look upon as a triumph for all revolutionaries, and a real motive for rejoicing amidst the setbacks we have had to endure.

We offer you our fraternal greetings together with the certainty of further successes in the common revolutionary task which we have set ourselves to achieve.

We send warmest greetings from all the comrades of the ELN.

MAY THE WAR CONTINUE!

VICTORY OR DEATH!

December 1970

Theoretical Writings

I Time and Politics[1]

Mastery of the Present: the Touchstone of Historical Materialism

The present situation and what we have to do: this anodyne, neutral, almost cliché of a heading both expresses and conceals what constitutes the essence of Marxism – what Marxism is all about. Just what is the relationship suggested by the 'and' in it? Certainly not just placing two things together: it is not a description (of the present situation) set alongside an exhortation (as to what we have to do). It is that the determining and organizing of the things we must do – of our line of action – takes place in view of an analysis of the situation. This does *not* however mean that the analysis is the premise, and the determining of what we must do the conclusion or consequence that flows from the premise. The relationship between the two is something more profound.

In a sense, *Capital* could be given a similar title. We tend to forget to what extent its real aim bears the seal of the *present moment*; the research, the immense documentation, the events brought under consideration, all relate to what was of the immediate present for Marx in 1867. But to say that something is 'of the present' does not mean that it is necessarily the thing most obviously in view. On the contrary, it was Marx himself who decided what was 'of the present' in his day: the development of productive forces and of capitalist relationships of production; and he saw that present reality as a movement, an ongoing process. To get some idea of the absolute originality (and no one since has attempted anything like it) of Book I, we might imagine a rigorous analysis of the same kind in our own day, considering the most recent technological, scientific, demographic, financial and political events, the latest trade statistics, the parliamentary statements of the past year or two, and so on, none of which we see as having

---

1. This piece was first published in *Les Temps Modernes*, June 1970.

any theoretical status, or even any particular significance, since these very disparate elements are not linked with any structure or organized movement which would account for their appearance at *this* moment or in *this* particular form.

'Questions of the moment': what is going on, what we see now, what surrounds us, enters into us, absorbs us. In this sense one has to put the phrase in quotation marks: it means the present reality of the newspapers, of our day-to-day world. But the essential problem for us is whether, and in what conditions, 'present reality' can be a scientific category at all. It then becomes 'the present moment' (Lenin), or 'the present situation' (Mao).

In this connection present reality is no longer an ontological category or a subject for consideration, but the *criterion* of a rational political view, the criterion for the existence of a practical political rationality. The present may be turned into a category, as *a priori* experience has been, but this then brings us back to the existential metaphysic. There is, after all, nothing illegitimate about such a return to experience, merely a shift of ground: we are reflecting upon human time, on the present as the fate of the experiencing subject (there can only be a present for an experiencing subject, and like the need for contingency it is a fate, as Sartre shows). We come then to 'being-for-death', the speculative recognition of that need which we have, and which must find practical expression, to live in a state of urgency, to live the present as an opportunity to be grasped, not to be missed, because the present can never be recaptured. Keynes's epigram about the long-term value of savings – 'In the long term, we shall all be dead' – only makes sense in one very definite historical context, the atheistic individualist West, but that context happens also to be objectively the fate of us all. In the long term, we and everything we do will be things of the past.

The basis from which we start is not the fact that there will always be a present for men, but the fact that the present never stays the same. 'Presentness' in general, the abstract fact of the present is neither an object for study nor a practical problem to solve; it is the stuff of literature, an artistic theme, a way of deepening our speculation about the human condition. On the other hand, the Marxist problem is to determine the present as a present situation, a singular and unique situation, a concrete situation. The Marxist problem is to know whether, and if so how, there can be any knowledge of the unique and exceptional, whether and how one can make an abstraction from the Aristotelian definition of science or the positivist definition of law.

To understand the scope of this problem, it must be seen from two aspects: it is an epistemological problem, and also a problem of political practice. On the one hand, Marxism must be examined as a science, on the other as a principle of [political guidance. And where the two meet the epistemological question is expressed as a practical question, and the political question as a scientific one; in other words what we are discovering now is the relationship and unity of the two questions. The refusal of the new Marxist scientism to look at this question (with its emphasis on the formal and general structures of the scientific approach), inevitably results in a kind of political absenteeism, a failure to enter into 'the present situation'; and it can only be interpreted as symptomatic of a failure in understanding, or rather of a refusal to face the question of unity, or relationship. What kind of 'science' is it which never leads to an analysis of the present historical situation – in all its complexity, its various levels, its special inequalities, and so on? What kind of political analysis, what adoption of a line of action, is it that is not supported by the use of scientific concepts or the application of any abstractly articulated theoretical instrument?

Seizing hold of the 'now' of history (in a given country, at a given time, though of course it also involves a seizing of the international relationships prevailing in the rest of the world at a given time, just as it implies a knowledge of all the previous history of the country itself) serves as a kind of touchstone for the theoretical validity of 'science', as well as a baptism of fire for the theorist himself. If that 'now' is not intellectually mastered, then the fundamental problem of 'What is to be done?' has no basis and no answer. To master it calls for a considerable preliminary knowledge, a necessarily abstract theoretical apprenticeship; but if that knowledge and apprenticeship do not ultimately provide an ability to take a grasp on the here and now, then we shall have lost the only guarantee now existing that one day the masses will become the masters of their fate, will pass out of the rule of necessity into that of freedom (the necessity being what is expressed in social planning), and no longer remain in the wings of the stage on which their fate is being acted out. If our present is not intelligible, then communism is a utopia: there is no more a scientific politics, no more a possibility that the process of history may be guided by a force that is aware of its position in 'present conditions'; the future stops being a task facing us, and becomes the whim of God. And God is a constant threat. If we lose our understanding of the present, then we also lose our future, and ultimately our very status as a zoological species: will the history of *homo sapiens* ever be more than a part of natural history?

'Time', noted Trotsky by the way, commenting on the errors made in the International after Lenin, 'is an important factor in politics.' I should prefer to say that it is not just a factor, but the dimension within which all the factors are seen and take effect. Not one factor like the rest, but the factor of factors: time is to politics what space is to geometry. The metaphor may not be worth much if we stick at Euclid; but relate it to modern geometries, where each has its own space. Time is clearly not a homogeneous continuum; each period of social development, each social grouping has its ups and downs in time (though still programmatic, this is understood today, as by Althusser), and so on. Political time moves faster in periods of crisis, and stagnates in times of regression: we learn more in a week of revolution than in ten years of *status quo*; and so on. But if we think of time in terms of what is of the moment or not of the moment, as the adaptation of a political line to a situation, then we see that adaptation as consisting in choosing the *right objective*. The science of objectives is the science of what is relevant to the moment; what was still right yesterday can become quite wrong today: recognizing what is different about oday, in what respect today is not yesterday, means recognizing what is special about the present moment, identifying that moment's unique, characteristic, distinct features.

Good political leadership works in with a dialectical time, in other words development of contradictions which, though irregular, open out into a series of stages or phases, variable in length (a week, a month, a few hours, or several years) but relatively homogeneous, and each having a characteristic and fundamental element distinguishing it from the previous stage of (temporary) resolution. It is therefore necessary to recognize and identify the point at which each stage is reached and passed, without losing sight of the general movement of that continuing process which unceasingly alters the relationship of forces in one direction or the other. This can only be done by having one's hand on the pulse of the process. One must react quickly; one needs a kind of second sense for recognizing change, and sensing the novelty of the question put by each period as one enters it in order to give an adequate answer. Leninism is just that capacity for making sudden, sharp turns, changing one's tactics as and when the situation changes. 'The art of waging the political battle' – Lenin's own phrase – is the art of entering at precisely the right time an objectively ongoing process. Coming neither too soon nor too late, seizing the $\kappa\alpha\nu\rho\delta\varsigma$.

The time it takes to produce material things, or to carry out a mechanical task, is a homogeneous quantity: what is lost by a work stoppage can be regained by an extra period at work; a piece cut from the beginning of the month can be added on at the end, the total not depending upon the individual factors. But from a political point of view, if a strike fails, if the most is not got out of it, it can never be made up for. 'It can sometimes take years and years to make up for lost months' (on the failure of March 1921 in Germany, see the splendid chapter 'Tradition and Revolutionary Politics' in *The New Course*, Trotsky, first published in Russian in 1924). Trotsky too, at about the same time, put forward the notion that if Lenin had not impressed the enthusiasm of the April theses on the Bolshevik Party, and if six months later he had not been able to overcome the 'general wavering' of the organs of leadership, and force the October breakthrough, then the takeover of power would have been postponed certainly for an indefinite period, and possibly forever. Kerensky was preparing a compromise peace with the Germans who, had they demobilized the Army would have demobilized the most formidable concentration of the masses ever seen (there were three to four million peasants and workers among the troops at the front); Kornilov was still of use; the Constituent Assembly would soon meet again; and so on. Lenin never denied this theory.

The Speculative Concept of Historical Time: the Mainstay of Reformism

Comments of this kind leave us with a concept of time that totally contradicts common sense. To paraphrase the Ninth Thesis on Feuerbach, one could say that, as opposed to speculative materialism, dialectical materialism conceives the time of social development as a practical activity, and not a factor that can be taken in isolation, a neutral parameter of development. We know that there is a conservative theory of time, characterized by the notion of inevitable decadence, of moral and social degradation, of a progressive growth away from origins. Time is a slope which we can only roll down: to prevent that happening, we must 'react', must hold fast and preserve what can be saved. But we are not sufficiently aware that 'time' in revolutionary dialectic is not the level time of reformism, though one cannot quite go so far as to declare that the two have nothing in common at all, since they share the same ideological heritage: the Enlightenment belief in progress, which in spite of everything, and more or less unconsciously, supports a number of para- or peri-Marxist formulae. Reformist time advances by gains and losses, additions and subtractions. Gain and loss are reckoned in relation to a total which already exists in theory and whose reality is projected for the future; addition and subtraction in relation to a result which will also be achieved in the future, but which rebounds on the present. A loss of votes in an election is seen as a step backward. What this apparently means is a step backward by comparison with the results of earlier elections, but in fact that step backward is experienced as a delay, a marking time or a temporary slip in relation to the final result which is seen as the end of the process: the absolute majority, or a majority large enough to lead to an alliance with the middle classes, the victory of the united front, the gradual achievement of socialism, etc.

Time is a road to be travelled more or less quickly, and we do not always get along as fast as we should like; but the point of arrival lies immutably at the end, fixed from the start. It is waiting for us. If there is an electoral defeat, we shall get there a bit later than expected; if there is a large increase in votes, an increase in party activists, party newspapers, party members elected to parliament, then we shall reach the end sooner because we have taken on a spurt of speed. The goal is set first of all, and working back from that, we calculate our position on the line by comparing the distance already covered with the distance that remains to be covered. Reformism's accounts are always clear because basically they go backwards. In this businesslike wait for the end, for the Great Evening, which may be nearer or further away but which is always certain to come finally, what we are seeing is the old religious attitude, though hidden beneath the most profane, the most 'scientific' of apparatus. This electoralist mistake really conceals the heresy of the millennium. The monster of German social democracy (monstrous in size, that is) which led the Second International, and dominated the European workers' parties at the beginning of the century by the efficiency of its mass organizations, the numbers of its members (more than a million!), and the skill of its leaders, made a point of cultivating memories of the peasant wars of the sixteenth century, but it did not draw from them the lessons that Engels drew. Kautsky made an excellent bedfellow for Münzer and the Utopianist Melchiorites of Münster, not so much in strengthening national traditions (which Engels did too, hoping to give Germany a revolutionary tradition as fine as that of France, especially since the defeat of 1848), or in

exalting the nation's heroism, but because hope for the kingdom
of Zion at the end of this vale of tears is familiar to that patience
which reformism has raised to the status of a theoretical argument.

Nor must one forget the importance of one immediate historical
factor in the unconscious formation of speculative time which
belongs to all mechanistic theories and practices. For the German
social democracy of the time, the absence of any actual experience
of socialism before 1917 resulted in the illusion that there was
indeed a clearly marked out 'line of arrival', coinciding with the
conquest of power by the Party, beyond that line all contradictions,
all trials, all the deceptive tricks of pre-history would disappear,
and a new world would open up that was utterly different from
the old hell of capitalism. Since then, as a series of socialist States
has been set up, people have had to learn that no such line existed,
that the race was never finally won, and even, and indeed above
all, that the class struggle does not unfold along a single straight
line according to a road laid out beforehand. The changeover in
the organization of political power does not automatically coincide with a changeover in the social relationships of production
(there is a difference between *de jure* state ownership, and *de facto*
ownership of the means of production by the people, between
decrees of nationalization and effective social management, and
so on); still less does it coincide with the kind of total about-face
in the ideology of the masses, in morality, in forms of awareness
and social behaviour, which alone makes it possible to speak of a
'before' and an 'after'. People had also to learn that a new series
of contradictions emerged within socialism itself, and that even
between socialist countries national disputes could develop into
antagonism and war.

None of this experience of history was available to the fundamentally mystagogical (social democrat) workers' movement of
the first decades of the century. Working backwards from the end
became harder, since the whole notion of an end of any kind was
brought into doubt – whether it took the form of a Parousia (the
Kingdom, Happiness in another world), an arithmetical end (the

final sum of gains, votes and seats in parliament when all added together), or a historical one (a once and for all irreversible achievement, the end of a period in world history). Whatever form it may take, such a concept of historical time has not disappeared and can perhaps never fully disappear. We must recognize that it is something to which we hold with the utmost tenacity in the depths of our being, or rather which holds us. Nonetheless we must recognize the opiate element in this ideological compound (which has all the power and reality of the imaginary); we may really find we need some analgesic to soothe the pains and anxieties of our work, but let us not dignify that opiate with the name of science.

The first supposition runs thus: historical time is endowed with a spontaneous faculty for accumulation. Each of its periods (time can be divided, according to the desired unit, into homogeneous and successive portions) accumulates elements the addition of which makes it possible to advance to a higher stage, a superior stage of social development. There is a way in which this concept is implanted by the capitalist–industrial theory of time. Capital is the accumulation of labour. Living labour, the product of dead labour, has become solidified into fixed capital: this accumulation process is indefinite; there is always more at the end than at the beginning. So victory will result from political work as it mounts up over a longer or shorter period, in the form of the Party's experience, the way it becomes gradually more established, the number of people voting for it, the solidity of its infra-structure, and so on, the sum total of which constitutes a kind of fixed capital: what the movement has accumulated since its origin. In this kind of accounting there have sometimes to be subtractions; there are times when voters are lost, when a newspaper has to close down, when the class enemy wins a point or two, and so on. But such subtractions are only temporary. Since nothing can ever be really lost, we shall in some sense recover at the end whatever we may have lost on the way: the subtraction is only *de facto*, never *de jure*. The movement in general will always recoup such losses. History knows its own. A loss is the temporary, artificial, often deceptive facet of an inevitable gain which is only in concealment or suspense for a time.

The practical conclusion from this is that nothing is irrecoverable.

The second supposition runs thus: the movement of history is determined by its end; in other words, the end is seen as fulfilling the role of the classic goal; the notion of the goal is the cause of what is really happening, providing unity and coherence for thousands of local movements, with the advances, the interruptions and the imperceptible gains through which the general movement is concretely embodied. Just as the history of the past is written by seeing what happened before in the light of what we now know to be its later developments, so the future we know becomes part of a past present which did not then know it ; similarly we turn our own present history into the 'past' of a future we think of as an achieved fact. In other words, this self-creating totalization necessarily relates to an ideal totality, which we consider as though it already existed, and which functions as the support and guarantee of the totalization now in progress. To believe that history creates itself, by means of certain additions and subtractions, means accepting that it is already complete. What is *not yet* is held in being by what *is already*. Of course we recognize the impress of Hegel (even though it be via Condorcet), the faith in progress of the great lights who play the leading parts. The ideal totality, or the idea of totality, ensures the infallibility of the empirical process of totalization. No one then (leaders, activists, even the masses) can fail in any radical way, or rather, failure can only be by default. A political mistake has no special positive effect, only a negative one: it may slow down the process, hamper it, set it off course perhaps, but it cannot affect its nature. Any error made is always something inessential.

The practical conclusion from this is that nothing is irremediable.

Thus I sum up in brief, and in necessarily philosophical terms, the postulates of our common attitude – our minimal dose, if you like, of opium. The political force of what may be called reformism, which remains persistent in spite of everything, weighs heavily upon our attitude and its weakness. 'Reformism' is an irresistible temptation, arising out of our cowardice. But let us get back to earth.

The Trap of Reformism: Crisis Situations

In Germany, for instance, because mention has been made of it, a lesson is to be drawn from what became in fifty years the most powerful working-class and Marxist movement in Europe. It was widely rooted by the end of the nineteenth century (the Second International was founded in 1889) in the homeland of scientific socialism. It is bad taste to recall the history of German socialism: could it be that there are truths best left unspoken? We all have some history we should prefer to be forgotten. There are some dates better not quoted: for socialists July 1914 is one such (just as in respectable French bourgeois families no one speaks of May 1940. Thousands of frightened soldiers scattered over the country-side like rabbits, with generals in the forefront – and if 'France' is to continue in existence, then *that* simply must not have happened. They were betrayed by incompetents, so the ruling class tell us). For us, 'the renegade Kautsky' betrayed the cause. Unfortunately, after that came January 1933. Thälmann is a martyr, and Stalin is not a renegade. And today there is in the Federal Republic, that is two-thirds of Germany, nothing, or almost nothing.

It would be superficial to present the development and disappearance of the German workers' movement in these terms, for it is not a humorous story, but a tragic and massive odyssey which got nowhere (or what West Germans now admit to have been nowhere). There is no scope here to write a serious history of it: it involves the history of the entire international socialist movement and, ultimately, the history of the social conditions of the twentieth century as a whole. We may recall merely the ups and downs of its profile: an ascending line, the rise of social democracy up to the first war, then a fall in July 1914; a massive though uneven rise, then a fall in 1933, and destruction. There were two impressive attempts at 'totalization', but twice they came up against 'a crisis'; the sum did not add up as it should, and both expectation and common sense were flouted. In July 1914 the Basle Congress resolution remained a dead letter, the social democrats in the Reichstag voted to declare war, and the workers almost to a man identified with the nation at war. In January 1933, Hitler met von Papen in the house of Schröder the banker, and thenceforth the strongest communist party anywhere in capitalist Europe was destined to disappear – not just in Dachau, but as far as the rank and file were concerned, in the crowds in Nuremberg. In 1969, on 1 May, the workers marched in the streets of West Berlin, of Cologne and of Hamburg, but they carried no red flag. When they saw a procession of left-wing students, one union leader was applauded as he shouted: 'In our Germany socialism isn't relevant any more.' Why?

The crisis of July 1914 put the national question in a special historical form. That vital question, which has traditional revolutionary Marxism continually pushed into the background ever since the time of Lenin – and in the event it has paid heavily for doing so – is not our concern here. The final post-war crisis in which Thälmann's party went down, and with it the independence of the working class, posed the problem of the dictatorship of financial capital or fascism and of the historical errors of the Communist International, a better known problem which has already been studied. But what the two crises have in common is having falsified all the expectations, routed the militants, caught the established leadership unawares – in other words, made a clean sweep. To common sense, to any non-dialectical view, a crisis situation is something appalling, a challenge to the intellect, a cause for ideological suspicion. This would not matter so much, were it not for another fact: that no one can have any practical mastery of a phenomenon of which he has no theoretical understanding, or more precisely of which he is from the start in no position to acquire any understanding.

The 'Why' of Historical Crises: Recalling the Dialectical Foundations

Historical time includes certain strategic points called 'crises'. They are 'epoch-making' events in the sense that they mark the culmination of one process and the beginning of another. The working-out of a crisis gives rise to a new situation, qualitatively distinct from the situation of the past. In the history of a society, passing from old to new does not happen through the addition or subtraction of separate elements, by an increase (of new elements into the totality of the past) or a diminution (of outworn elements); at a given moment in a continuing, latent, 'underground' process of transformation, there is an open crystallization on the surface of all the conflicting elements of history – a breaking-point, the critical moment, the crisis point. Then it is no longer possible to return to the balance of things as they were, but a new balance, superior and historically progressive by comparison with what went before, does not necessarily follow on from that. The decisive moment thus appears as a kind of chemical, disturbing, rapid precipitation of a mass of unforeseen events, experienced in uncertainty and confusion; its result remains uncertain. People who live through a crisis situation, whether political, social, military or a combination of them all, hour by hour, day by day, find it at once intensely clear and intensely confused. It is clear to everyone that something of vital importance is being determined, but no one can agree as to what the solution will be. 'Anything might happen' is the general feeling. In other words nothing is certain. It is a decisive moment yet at the same time undecided; it is essentially uncertain in its results, yet is subject to a total rational process; an indeterminate moment of determination; a solution which itself contradicts previous contradictions. Crises look utterly paradoxical to anyone who does not understand how their inevitable recurrence brings to light the concealed paradoxes of history itself; they are the pure and simple – i.e. impure and complex! – manifestation of the laws of social development.

The major exponents of dialectical materialism have worked out

in essence the nature, the means and the need for the periodic recurrence of 'crises' in all social development. Indeed that dialectic
itself could be described as fundamentally a theory of crises in
nature and society.

On the nature, the meaning and the need for the periodic recurrence of 'crises' in all social development, all that matters has
been said by the major representatives of dialectic materialism.
That dialectic itself can basically be considered as a theory which
itself interprets the crises within nature and society. Its foundation
is the law of contradiction inherent in all phenomena – whether
objective or subjective, and the specific characteristics attributed
to that law by non-Hegelian Marxist-scientific or *materialist*
dialectic. (One may cite the example of the characteristics of
materialist contradiction as brought together by Mao Tse-tung in
1937 in which he rejected dogmatism and an automatic imitation
of the Russian example, and determined to work out an autonomous, specifically Chinese line.) The theory of the unity of opposites (which is what defined dialectic as far as Lenin was concerned)
calls for a theory of crisis as a special and necessary case. What
looks like unity conceals the presence of a split; what looks like
contradiction conceals the solidarity and unity of opposing
sections. In unity there remains a continual battle of contraries
right up to the point when the existing unity breaks apart, to give
birth to a new unity, in which a new series of contraries battle, and
so on. The moment of the break-up is what we may call the crisis,
the confrontation between contraries, the point of articulation between two unities, two periods of history, two political or social
régimes, two relationships between stable forces. Even a temporary
forgetfulness of the fundamental law of contradiction will make
the move from stability to instability, from tranquillity to agitation,
from balance to imbalance, look like a mere incident, an arbitrary
event resulting from some external cause which has no organic
connection with the process in question. The external cause,
whether a foreign intervention, a dangerous agitator, a subversive
agent, or whatever, thus becomes responsible for the crisis, and the
only way to resolve the crisis will be to defuse that cause. A meta-

physical or mechanistic concept of the world is bound to see any questioning of its world-view as a thunderclap in a cloudless sky. That is why metaphysicians have to have an active and vigilant police force to get rid of all external agents, and why in every officer of the bourgeois repression a metaphysician lies dormant. Underlying the problem of 'crises' and their control, do we not find the old metaphysical enigma: how can the same thing become something other? How can an object, a phenomenon, be transformed into its opposite – capitalism into socialism, national oppression into national liberation, a dominant class into a dominated class, and so on? We all know the answer: every object, every phenomenon, contains within itself its opposite; the struggle between the two facets of each specific contradiction (within the object or phenomenon under consideration) constitutes the mainspring of that object or phenomenon's development. The solution of the contradiction marks the end of a stage in that development, but as the next phase appears, a new form of contradiction at once becomes apparent; and this process is indefinite. Only death brings it to an end, since the law of contradiction is coextensive with life itself. Therefore the arrival of socialism certainly cannot be expected to mark the end of contradictions in history; Lenin pointed that out even before the Bolshevik revolution. But he may not have realized how profoundly true it was, because he did not allow for the possibility that such contradictions might, within a socialist world, take the form of antagonism, of actual open crisis and violent confrontation.

Thus, inside all balance, stability and cohesion, there is imbalance, instability and fragmentation. The cause of the crises and (qualitative) changes which affect or overtly threaten every state of balance, stability or cohesion is therefore not something exterior, but is written into their very nature in that perpetual (quantitative) transformation which is part of that nature. This does not of course mean that we can exclude the intervention of external, coincidental, incidental causes. But such external causes can only work through the intermediary of the internal, structural, essential causes which constitute the determining element in society's crises. That oldest ally of metaphysical repression, 'common sense', were it to carry its platitudes to their final conclusions would no doubt agree: after all, a perfectly healthy man does not have an epileptic fit as a result of an emotional shock. The paid journalists and other minions of imperialism are unmoved by the thought that 'Peking money' or 'Castro's agents' find their way into Switzerland or Denmark.

The 'How' of Crises: an Outline Description

Bearing in mind these elementary principles, and if we can (though it involves the danger of rendering all discussion meaningless) abstract the concrete conditions and special nature of the contradictions at work within any given situation, which impose the special historical form of the solution of the crisis, then we are obliged immediately to make several series of comments.

1. At the political level, which is the level at which crises appear, develop and are determined, changes in our experience of time (or in the intensity of objective time) depend on the rhythm of development of the contradictions in the formation-processes of society. That rhythm of development depends in turn on the degree of fusion in the contradictions (or their 'over-determination'); the crisis point occurs when at a given point (in the world: a given country at a given time, as Russia in 1917, or the university situation in France in 1968, etc.) the fusion culminates in a collapse of the old balance. A crystallization of contradictions results in a time of intense political activity, which has a chain reaction on other links which are less 'over-determined' at the moment than the link where the break happens. As against the slower-moving political time when the contradictions are ripening, so to speak, there is the rapid, explosive, convulsive time of breaking-up, when antagonisms reach crisis point. But the break-up is only apparent; there is no real fracture, for a time of crisis is simply ordinary time concentrated – just as, in Lenin's phrase, politics is simply concentrated economics. The movement of time is absolute and con-

tinuous, but does not always take the same form; its commonest form is one of apparent immobility. But in moments of concentration its true nature appears, and we see it for what it is as a struggle between opposites. Che described revolutions as 'When the extraordinary becomes the everyday'. But, one may add, the extraordinary *is* simply the everyday, concentrated and self-revealed: a moment of general political crisis brings to light the extraordinary elements hidden in the depths of the everyday class struggle at the economic or ideological level. The time of crisis suspends all ordinary norms, overthrows habits, and breaks all the accepted rules of behaviour, but it is only then that we see what the rule is, and that all the camouflage which hid the evidence of the struggle from the opponents falls away. It is as if the rule (the regulation of society's movement by its class struggles) can only be seen in its exception. Whatever may be said of such transformations, discontinuity or 'crisis' and the continuity of 'normal time' must both be seen in relation to their common basis so as to be seen through one another – the one regulating the other, so that both become intelligible. Each borrows its specific intelligibility from the other, as two moments in a single process.

2. The critical moment of fusion (or the explosion, i.e. the revelation, of contradictions which have accumulated to the point of overt antagonism) thus brings to the surface, to the level of open, political and public struggle, a break that spreads outwards, a split that soon extends to all the levels of the social totality it touches. There is a division into camps (classes and class blocs), boundaries are established between the collective actors – parties or political leaders (friends or enemies?), and eventually all this results in a demarcation *by* the crisis between the periods of the process taking place (the end of an old movement and beginning of a new). But this lightning-division, so rapid and spontaneous as to appear almost mechanical, merely rearranges the scattered forces of the old structures in the straightforward pattern of an opposition, a duel, a division into two, by accentuating and sharply defining their hitherto latent characteristics. In this way a crisis presents a readily understandable, clearly contrasted picture:

there is an arena of objective forces, of ideological tendencies, of leading personalities. In the photographic sense of the word, it gives us a good 'definition' of history. But this fact of bringing ambiguities into relief, and doing away with the apparent fluidity of the political outlines of social forces and individuals, their overlapping areas of non-determination, is costly. By encroaching on the edges, it narrows the central pathway, reducing the possibilities, the potentialities so to speak, of history. *Ad augusta per angusta.* It starts with a kind of bottle-neck. A serious political crisis presents itself in the constricting form of a dilemma: it is 'now or never' (never being an indefinite and probably far-off future); 'one thing or the other' (revolution or counter-revolution; in electoral terms, the centre is narrowed to nothing). Such are the rhetorical, extreme and sometimes illusory forms of actual alternatives which are obviously nothing like so clear-cut. We are left with a hardening of choice, the impossibility of remaining neutral, the inability to modify our course in the light of any new logic; we have reached 'an escalation to the extreme'. The struggle for domination is out in the open, and admits of no pretence. Once the principal contradiction has become evident as such, each of the two aspects in the crisis is either turned upside down or consolidates its position, either dominates or is dominated. A crisis makes clear precisely what is at stake. The critical point of the crisis determines on which side the scales come down.

3. Now this is the paradox: though it is the moment which resolves a contradictory process, a crisis appears as something infinitely problematical. Though it 'solves the question', it is itself a fearful question; in dividing, it tends to simplify; in point of fact it constitutes a complex of historical factors so interwoven, so varied and so confused that all the legions of politicians, dialecticians and theoreticians of Marxism – however sure of their positions – always find themselves completely at sea, and this is true of every decisive crisis, today as in the past. Though a crisis marks the instant at which the internal dialectic within a determined history comes fully to light, it itself is, so to speak, over-determined and unclear. In every crisis situation there is a typical

interplay of darkness and clarity. Those experiencing it, the two camps whom it brings into confrontation, see no very obvious or simple formula for resolving the crisis. The objective conditions provide a background, a containing framework of propositions, which restricts the spectrum of possible initiatives or responses to events, but that background then seems to withdraw, as it were, to fade, to become neutralized so as dramatically to throw into relief the inventive capacities and conscious activities of political movements. So much so that the outline, the thing that can be seen by everyone, shifts from the objective to the subjective, the indeterminate, with the individual initiatives of a few characters suddenly thrust into the forefront of the stage.

It is precisely because it appears in terms of a dilemma, an alternative, a leap to one extreme or another, that the crisis situation so sharply accentuates the power of decision of the leaders or those in authority. Never have they appeared more free, yet never have they in fact been so restricted; their room for manoeuvre is narrow, but for that very reason their decisions will have far-reaching effects. In one sense, their powerlessness in the face of events confers on them an increase of power and the 'aura' of power, of sovereignty, of responsibility. But their liberty is deceptive: where the roads divide, they have only to know which of two sets of mechanisms to set going, which inevitable sequence of events is to be yielded to with enough clearsightedness and resolution to be able to some extent to control the surge forward and appear to be guiding it. At the point where the ways divide (right or left, resistance or capitulation, dictatorship by one camp or the other, perhaps a choice between two deaths – two ways of dying for individuals or two forms of defeat for policies, but even the latter are never of precisely equal worth, and some choice must still be made), at that point one has to leave one road and take the other. At such moments, the signposts along the paths of history are generally concealed or non-existent. They only become visible later to critics and historians. Warning signs are always put up too late: notices saying 'Caution', 'Danger', 'Reduce speed' – or even perhaps 'Accelerate here' – are erected after the accident has happened, when they no longer serve any purpose, or rather when their only purpose is to jog society's memory; they are a 'history lesson'.

Thus if there is a choice (and refusing to make a choice is itself a choice) one can only opt for what seems the lesser of two evils. Furthermore it is not a deduction, but a gamble, in other words a well-judged leap in the dark. (I am not of course referring here to the pattern of the rules-of-the-game, which strictly applies only to games, implying in other words a certain number of restrictions accepted on both sides and clearly formulable. However, to transpose operational calculation on to the ground of the political class struggle, i.e. into entirely new and unique combinations of circumstances, presupposes an idealist conception of praxis as action quite disconnected from reward, non-dialectical and therefore in the last analysis ineffective – which means ineffective in the short term, since the short term is the mode of operation of all political practice.) The leap is rational in that it can produce its reasons; it is the end of a chain of reasoning, but an end reached only by way of a discontinuity, by crossing a gap in the reasoning itself; for if reasoning consists in an analysis of conditions as they are, as we perceive them, then we have made a leap beyond those present conditions, a leap into the future, an anticipation, in short a policy.

To make his anticipation as correct as possible by means of such analysis is the job of the politician as scientist. But to accept the risk of anticipating, and prove its correctness in action, is the job of the scientist as politician. There is necessarily a hiatus between these two levels. We may recall in this connection everything in Marx's attitude to the Commune, and the various letters to Kugelmann in April 1871; it was not chance that made Lenin write a preface to them in which he stressed their provocative and shocking nature. Indeed it would almost seem that Lenin positively relished stressing that hiatus. The same thing applies to The *Eighteenth Brumaire*, this time in the sardonic mode: in 1848, 'circumstances cried out: *hic Rhodus, hic salta* – this is Rhodes and it is from here that we must jump', and the democratic bourgeois either would not or could not make that forward leap, and were consequently obliged later to effect a whole series of little leaps, but backwards, until they came up against the final barrier of 2 December. A crisis situation seems to have imprinted within it the image of its special function in history as a whole: the destruction of the old unity by a leap into the new unity, a qualitative leap, a discontinuity by jumping from one era to the next, from a régime of domination by one class to domination by another.

Thus in itself, in its practical development, the general crisis represents a challenge to continuity, both in logic and in the sequence of actual events. There is a hiatus between the means available and the goal to be achieved (as in Russia for the Bolsheviks after the October Rising). There is a hiatus between what one can do and what one must do (at its worst, that hiatus becomes a political tragedy, the fatal excess of a Thomas Münzer, and of the failed peasant revolutions as analysed by Engels). In every decisive crisis there is an inevitable hiatus between the need to make a decision and the available information on which to base it rationally, a hiatus between the need to effect a choice at a given moment and the, to some extent inevitable, element of contingency in the conditions in which that choice must be made. There are certain exceptional moments when a complex process, already in being, is summed up and seen in its entirety in one simple alternative which will qualitatively transform the way the process is going in one direction *or* the other; the archetypal or mythical (though real enough to those living through it in the inevitable uncertainty of the immediate present) example of such a moment was the ten days before the October Rising, and the decision made by Lenin to move to an open attack on the power of the State.

There is a certain dizziness in every crisis; at a certain moment, the critical point of the crisis, there is an instant, a patch of total darkness (as during the famous night of Smolny which the Bolsheviks speak of in their memoirs), when there is a sense of emptiness and one remains as if suspended in the air, waiting for who knows what, for some sign, something to grasp hold of. Even the most resolute feel a sinking in their stomachs. What they feel is the gulf between the determined action which is seen to be necessary and unavoidable, and the theoretical conditions in which any such action becomes possible; these do not seem to have come together sufficiently to make the choice clear. Basically, what the crisis situation reveals is that the dialectical structure of history is always presented to us as a conjunction of circumstances; in other words what we are ultimately dealing with is necessity in the concrete form of contingency, however that contingency may be determined, and indeed *precisely because it is so*. (Althusser has explained this better than anyone in *Contradiction and Over-determination*, that most remarkable, most useful, and richest in concrete analysis of all his works: a certain mistaken passion for theorizing has since led him to wander off to heights of logic from which one can only wonder if he will ever be able to return to the political earth where we, poor blind mortals, are feeling our way in the half-light of the present, spurred on by the urgency of what we have to do.)

In politics it is sometimes rational to go beyond what is reasonable: only a single step forward, but it is more of a leap than a step. Philosophers, ideologues, all the inactive spectators or judges of history, are terrified of a void and incapable of making such steps, or even of understanding them except in retrospect. Those happy souls will never have that shiver of apprehension which Che, for instance, appears to have felt intensely before any decisive action involving an element of the unjustifiable; he probably felt it more acutely than anyone, given the detailed, mathematical keenness of his mind, his training as a thinker, and his extraordinary intellectual lucidity. But he was able then to stand completely outside himself, and, when the need arose to silence the theoretician, the analyst, the ' intellectual ' in himself, and hurl himself with wordless, impassive resolution into what must be done, into the thing that had been decided. The more uncertain the situation, and the more aware he was of its uncertainty, the more serene he remained. He saw more clearly than ¦anyone the doubts, the chances, the necessities, but once a decision was made, then danger merely strengthened his resolve more totally (like Marx when the 'bold folly' of the Commune had been unleashed, except that in Che's case he was actually there, in the front line). Really, in such moments when 'everything hangs on a thread ', the best service leaders can render those fighting with them is to remain calm. Confusion merely weakens the thread.

4. Though crisis is inevitable, there is no foretelling what its results will be. If we look at all the major crises of recent history which have led to decisive changes in capitalism, we may notice that in each one there has been something aberrant, imperfect, deviant. The 'genuine crisis', the ideal revolutionary crisis according to the book, should 'logically' correspond to the moment at which the kernel of productive forces begins to push against the constricting shell of production relationships. This regular and normal development would in due course, its period of gestation complete, lead not to an explosion but to the flowering of a new form of political organization corresponding to the necessary socialization of the means of production. In effect, if we compare the crisis situation which can give birth to a socialist revolution to the pains of childbirth, we may go on to say that the infant regularly emerges wrongly: it is expected to come head first, but instead comes feet first or sideways; it is premature, still-born or sickly. It is not what a perfect infant should look like, and that is why it is not always recognized for what it is. (The old socialists of the Second International, for instance, even the least revisionist among them, had a hard time recognizing the young Soviet republic of 1917 as the copybook republic of their hopes.) This failure to conform to its own image, this inner wrongness, is precisely what constitutes the special nature of every genuinely new event in living history. The progress of the Hegelian Spirit towards its fulfilment by way of geographical, racial, economic, religious and other contingencies should not surprise us at all.

If the idea were replaced by the simple contradiction: productive forces versus production relationships, then it would make it possible to produce a triumphant, pre-determined, punctilious progress of the economic essence through all the phenomena of politics, and every political crisis would be a healthy crisis of growth. Malfunctionings and abortions are simply by-products of development, its rough edges, if you like. We know in fact that the aberrant or abnormal quality (by the standard of our abstract norms) of crisis situations, of concrete revolutionary situations, is due precisely to the fact that there has to be a unique fusion of contradictions, in which the basic or economic contradiction itself becomes determined by a welter of elements of all kinds, which bring it to its breaking-point. That breaking-point is not generally heralded in advance by the kind of definite determinations which make it possible to identify it directly – the history of revolutions is not so nicely behaved. We did not expect it from that direction, or at that time, or in that form. It upsets all our plans and pre-arranged strategies, catching up on them from behind; and very often, in its suddenness, a crisis interrupts and thus spoils what seemed a 'favourable' political development. The leaders then get the sense that their hand is being forced, because a crisis pushes them into making choices, following lines, making certain breaks that they deplore. Crises, with their actor-victims, never radiate glory, never appear as great historical necessities. As far as one can judge over half a century, when that Great Night does come, whenever it may be, it seems more like a cold and misty dawn. The epic only comes into being in retrospect. There is something irritating, from any religious or apocalyptic standpoint, in the unexpected breaking out of a major revolutionary crisis. From the standpoint of the headlines, the upheavals are a disappointment. There is no end to the tiresomeness of history as it actually occurs; even in the victories, triumph always comes mingled with defeat.

Like the social totality which it affects through and through, like the collision of contradictions which make it possible, the crisis situation when it comes is complex. In an 'organic crisis', the simplification of the battlefield of the classes is achieved by means of an extreme complexity, or combination of objective factors

independent of our wishes. It is in that very contradiction that
the crisis drama develops: the will or conscious activity of individuals is called for by simple, simplifying demands, but intellectually they must grasp the situation of the moment in all its
complexity (where it comes from; what has made it possible; the
fundamentals it reveals in the position of the classes or sections of
classes *vis-à-vis* one another, and so on). On the one hand, a crisis
simplifies the field of practical politics by forcing us into a
straightforward dilemma, a choice between two opposites pushed
to their furthest extremes; on the other, it reveals bit by bit the
tangles, the combinations, the inter-dependence of all its constituent elements. There are no nuances at all in the things it
forces us to do : ultimately it is the White terror or the Red, defeat
or victory, open rebellion or going underground. But the way in
which it develops brings into play a large number of factors which,
if looked at closely, can be seen to be unsteadily bound together:
consider Lenin's account of the combination of internal and
international causes which made the October Rising possible and
enabled it to survive. A crisis is a knot that cannot be untangled,
but must be cut. We must try to untangle it in theory, or at least
more or less intuitively grasp its complexity, but only so as to be
able to make practical decisions that will bring it to a successful
conclusion by resolutely simple, even simplistic-seeming, formulae
for action. In 1917, Lenin's agrarian programme was expressed in
a few sentences, and they were a shortened version of something
taken from the Social Revolutionaries. His political programme
was only three words: peace, land and bread. But though they
might look like three words of mere generalization, they are in
fact dense in meaning, and they went straight to the heart of the
crisis situation by pointing the way to steps that could be taken
immediately: negotiations, redistribution of land, and economic
requisitioning. That is the famous 'simplism' of the Bolshevik
slogans – the simplicity not of abstraction, but of condensation.
In condensed form they give a concrete analysis of a concrete
situation, so in fact they contain a wealth of possible determinations. It is this that gave them their explosive force and enabled

them to have such an effect on the masses. They were based on quite precise realities outside themselves, elements in the total combination of circumstances prevailing at the time. They were not the kind of clichés we get treated to in after-dinner speeches about such vaguely fine things as peace, happiness, democracy and general disarmament. Such high-sounding words have nothing to do with communism. What turns a well-meaning phrase into a genuine political aim is its capacity to act as a lever, in other words to use the present moment, accurately assessed, as a springboard. We need no more heart-warming commemorative plaques on cathedral walls!

There is no such thing as history in general, or crisis in general. But one thing that is common to all crisis situations is that they *obstruct* all our normal perspectives. The new cuts a path across the old in such a way that, when the crisis occurs, it seems to open out into a dead-end. Such is the evident end of the 'Nevski prospect' which, as Lenin foretold, had no bearing on the course of history. The direct road eventually ends in a cul-de-sac, which is why one must turn either to right or to left, or perhaps take a leap forward or go backwards, but one way or another, change direction. That is how a crisis looks from close up, when one is actually involved in it. But in fact things are always less critical than they seem at any given time. History tends to work its way round obstacles rather than confront them squarely, and over the course of time these emerge unexpected and complicated solutions for solving 'insoluble' problems through long-term compromises. But, in the short term, Lenin was quite right in his description of the general crisis of the capitalist system at the end of the First World War: 'These are the objective conditions which have come together as a result of the imperialist war, and which have brought all of mankind into the impasse of the following dilemma: *either* to let millions more people perish and annihilate European civilization, *or* to hand over power to the revolutionary proletariat in all civilized countries, and thus achieve the socialist revolution.'

(Twenty years later another crisis, another world war, presented us with an equally clear-cut alternative, expressed in a phrase more moral than political: 'Socialism or Barbarism'. Nazism was crushed, but, though it may not be kind to say so, history in capitalist Europe eluded the dilemma after the war, by slightly shifting the emphasis of the two terms, by making socialism somewhat barbarous, with Stalin, and his cult, and by to some extent socializing capitalist barbarism with pension funds and some token planning. Periods of relative stability, the long periods preceding or following the crises, come to look like an attempt to combine or work out compromises between contradictions. These are what might be called the mongrel periods of history. But they are necessary.)

Thus there is an imbalance in a crisis situation: objectively over-determined, while subjectively indeterminate (relatively speaking, of course – relative to the existing conditions: the ritual 'everything is possible' is precisely the subjective illusion that characterizes moments of crisis). That is the first dramatic element: the imbalance, in a sense, provides the mainspring of the 'suspense'.

The second consists in the sudden contraction of past and future times into the present, forming a kind of knot linking together times that would ordinarily be quite separate. A crisis sums up a complex past, and prefigures a period still to come. There is a flattening of perspectives: the distant is placed up against the near, in the forefront. It is here that the solution of the crisis, the line adopted, the way people behave at that moment may be said to be decisive: they determine the way things will go for a long time to come. The decision taken at that moment is a long-term one. What is dramatic in every crisis is the sudden telescoping of time. What must be done must be done at once, but what is done will also have effects that ramify over a long period. There is the shortest possible gap between the strategic plan and the tactical one. In fact the strategy appears as tactics, *all its force is directly tactical*, the two become as one. We can no longer draw on future credit: the present is now (because now is when it is being determined). Strategy must be paid for in cash, so to speak, in decisions to be taken at once. There is no way out. Hence the intensity of the 'crisis moment', the profound density of every least word, of every silence, even of inaction. So great is the over-determination that everything has a meaning, even nothingness – indeed especially nothingness and absence (as with the disappearance of de Gaulle at the end of May 1968; but de Gaulle was a strategist of genius, and all the more so in that he was then fighting against 'ordinary men', leaders who were not made for crises because they were not made leaders *in* crises as de Gaulle himself had been).

This particular density results from:

a) the fact that what is at stake is probably condensed into a single point in social time and space. In wartime, that stake is the very survival of the nation. At other times it may be the survival of a political régime, the direction in which a period of history is moving, etc. That stake affects a *totality*, or, more precisely, it is the risk, the very indecision that makes the elements at stake into a *kind of totality*. 'Everything' depends on a single decision, on the result of a single battle, the success of a single manoeuvre. It is for this reason that the affair is strategically decisive; in itself it may be minute, quite insignificant, quite ridiculously unimportant, but its importance is strategic in that the totality in question is wholly present in it (or, once again, over-determines it). The battle of Valmy was a military outing at trotting speed – no more – but none the less decisive for that. The battle of Eylau was a massacre, but strategically useless. In every political or military event what matters is not the thing in itself, but its relationship to its context. In themselves, the barricades in the Latin Quarter were a joke. It was their concrete connection with a symbolic period (May 1968), with an economic situation and with the struggles of the workers, which made them politically decisive. This connection itself was only possible because of the presence of certain specifically French features (the role of the 'intellectual', absent in England and Germany, plus revolutionary traditions; a collective mirage, plus, above all, the existence of a combative and politicized working class); and of social, political and economic conditions which will never again occur together in precisely the same way. In this sense the barricades in the Latin Quarter were, politically, built from outside (from the French past and from factories in outlying areas). All that had to be done at that point and in that place was physically to put them up.

b) the disproportion, in the effectiveness of political actions, of cause and effect, a clear reflection of this same density. One mistake, one false step, one error that would not normally matter at all, may become irreparable in a time of crisis, because it occurs in the place and at the time the condensation is happening. It is hard to control this amplifying of effects and re-percussions (as witness Mitterrand's press conference, referring again to May 1968). The over-significance of the spoken word reflects the over-determination of the crisis. The paradox is that there is at once an increased margin for initiative, for free action, and a reduced tolerance of error. In this sense every crisis presents a trap.

There is another element that is dramatic – that is to say not mechanistic or fatalist: though the peculiar function of a crisis is to define the possible camps and 'coups', on one side and the other of a given demarcation line, each camp involved has to make a choice, but that choice is not an inevitable one. (It goes without saying that by 'choice' I mean the application or adoption of one line, and the consequent rejection of the opposite line which would have been just as possible; I do not mean the conscious decision of a single moment or act.) It is a difficult choice, being neither the Manichean option between two moral entities, nor one that appears logically obvious. The road forks, but both directions involve danger, and it is just that measured comparison and assessment of the risks that is made impossible by the urgency of the crisis. What may be judged in the short term as the lesser risk may, seen in the perspective of the long term, appear as the greater. Yet in the confused immediacy of the crisis we become incapable of seeing that long-term perspective. If we can manage to get back to it, we generally come to a result that, to those who have been taken in by the mirage of the short-term view, appears paradoxical, indefensible, completely adventurist.

The Example of 1871 and the Dispute between Marx and Kugelmann

Marx's support of the Commune was at once enthusiastic and resigned. Having expressed admiration for the Parisians and their 'storming heaven', in which he and Kugelmann were wholly of one mind, it remained to make a political assessment of the risks involved, and this was the crux of their differences, the crux of the action. Kugelmann, the typical 'fine militant', thoughtful, steady, sincere, took the negative view, the rising was premature because it ignored the logical order of time whereby there must first of all be political education, then organization and only after that action: 'The defeat will once again deprive the workers of their leaders for quite a long time. That is a misfortune which cannot be overestimated! In my opinion, the proletariat for the moment needs education far more than armed struggle.'[1] Marx replied sharply, but somewhat obliquely, by re-phrasing the question. Fundamentally he too expected defeat, and was in tacit agreement with his correspondent on this point. In his letter of 17 April, he replied (I summarize):

a) that history would be 'of a very mystical nature' if it imposed tasks for which all the conditions for success were always infallibly present together;

b) that though in the short term the conditions for fighting were unfavourable, not to have fought would, in the long term, have created still more unfavourable conditions for the battles to come;

c) that the rising, even though defeated, would mark a turning point, a 'new point of departure' in the history of the capitalist State and society. In these circumstances, given that the alternative is present *in the events*, it is better to take extra risks *now*, in order to avoid others, even more numerous and more serious, which may not appear until *later*. Marx takes as his basis the situation as it actually is; Kugelmann what it ought to be, what he

1. Taken from *The Eighteenth Brumaire of Louis Napoleon*; editor's note on p. 15 of the edition published by Éditions Sociales.

would have preferred it to be. Marx sees the present in the perspective of the future – the essential quality Gorki recognized in Lenin, indeed the essential quality of Leninism. Or more precisely: he sees it from the point of view of the future. But it is the present that decides; the present is the point of departure. Kugelmann preaches to the present from the point of view of a hypothetical, ideal future. He rejects the reality of the present moment in the name of his abstract evaluation of how things ought to be. He will not grasp the unity, the irreversibility of the moment.[1]

There is often something of Lenin in Marx, the later Lenin (the ironically Napoleonic Lenin who said: 'One first commits oneself and then considers'), especially during the crises of 1848 and 1871. In the heat of events we see something approaching *gauchisme*, an episodic voluntarism which seems to have taken possession of Marx during or just after the events that rocked Europe – an attitude in obvious contrast with the theoretical lines to be found in *Capital*, which follow Darwin almost word for word. That these two Marxes are one has still to be proved, for it is certainly far from evident.

The Example of 1914 and the Left of Zimmerwald

In Gorki's metaphor, the rightness of political action involves a kind of double vision: 'seeing' simultaneously what is near and what is distant, the near from the point of view of the distant.

1. From Marx's letter of 17 April 1871, to Kugelmann: 'The decisive unfavourable "accident" this time is by no means to be found in the general conditions of French society, but in the presence of the Prussians in France and their position right before Paris. Of this the Parisians were well aware. But of this, the bourgeois *canaille* of Versailles were also well aware. Precisely for that reason they presented the Parisians with the alternative of taking up the fight or succumbing without a struggle. In the latter case, the demoralization of the working class would have been a far greater misfortune than the fall of any number of "leaders".' Karl Marx, *Selected Works*, vol. 2, p. 531, London, 1943.

To adapt properly to the present moment presupposes situating it in the total on-going process, recognizing that it contains the future in dialectical form; grasping the point of connection, the point of entry of the objective in view, the goal to be achieved at the present juncture. This achievement of a theoretical-cum-intuitive perspective may well result in sharp *changes* of perspective in one's current assessment of risks which should or should not be run at a given moment. Take July 1914 for example. From a strategic point of view – by which of course I mean an abstract point of view – the terms are not posed in this way, indeed they are not posed at all, since there is a complete eclipse of all theoretical statements of the problems, and the leaders are carried helplessly along in the whirlwind, barely even aware of the dozens of pacifist resolutions, congresses, statements, that they are forgetting. From a strategic point of view, then, the crisis of war being declared meant that the Socialist International had to choose between illegality, with treason trials, internal divisions, and the loss of some of its best members on the one hand, or preserving the existing organizations, though at the cost of becoming involved in the imperialist war, the 'sacred union', chauvinism, and so on. Had they in fact had to make a choice, had they had the time to weigh the options before them, had the crisis been such as to allow of deliberation and decision, had they been able to meet together round a table, the leaders of the International would have found themselves in the position of choosing between the present and the future, between an estimate of short-term losses and gains as against long-term ones. Opportunism means concentrating on immediate gains, mistaking tactics for strategy; the opportunist must at all costs avoid getting into the restricted position, or sharp turn of direction, or even perhaps the kind of dead-end in which he might be forced to commit himself to immediate action in order to create conditions that will be favourable in the long term.

By acting otherwise Lenin and his group appeared to almost all socialists to be behaving with utter lunacy, to be cutting themselves off from the masses, and falling prey to a false idealism in their refusal to give approval to the war and to the massive support for the war all over Europe. But the Zimmerwald left group was not setting up an ideal against a fact – the ideal of proletarian solidarity or a negotiated peace, against the fact of the imperialist war; it took its stance firmly in circumstances as they were, but transformed them into a starting-off point, a springboard for getting *beyond* them towards the realization of 'the ideal' – the revolutionary programme. It was in no sense withdrawing from the actual situation, like those who wanted to return to the *status quo ante*, with peace and a return to the frontiers of pre-1914. It was not judging the real in terms of the ideal, or condemning the present in terms of some mythical future, like the Rolland-style pacifists. It was connecting the future to the present by in a sense doubling the stake: the only way to avoid the risk of disintegrating or being exterminated was to be prepared to accept the additional risk of the civil war. In other words, the solution must not be sought *in* the here and now, but through and beyond it. The actual situation was no longer something purely negative, helpless, hopeless – the imperialist war meaning the total shipwreck of all socialist ideals and programmes; seen in the new perspective, it became a half-opened gap through which, in new and more favourable conditions, an offensive revolutionary policy could come back into the picture.

Though it was a bold and long-term vision, Lenin had his feet on the ground; his vision was rooted 'in the conditions of the present'. Using those conditions as a springboard made it possible to leap in such a way that the leap appeared as a transformation of reality, a dialectical and plausible negation. For instance, the objective in this context became 'to change the imperialist war into a revolutionary civil war'. But this kind of 'change' owed nothing to Lamarck. It was not just that it was not a 'natural' progression, that it called for a power of decision; rather, if one studies the events of history, one can see it as an evident *transgression*: a leap forward across all the taboos and norms of 'ordinary life', and a complete break with the past, a break in historical continuity, a remodelling of the old line, and so on. In this, with its wealth of about-turns, surprises, zigzags, to adapt to changes in the situation, that disconcerting boldness, rapid and decided, is clearly very different from the mechanistic approach on its right. And it is just as different from the voluntarism or utopianism on its left, by the very fact of taking up its stance firmly in conditions as they are, of basing itself on objective reality as understood through correct analysis. That reality involves natural elements (the geographical position of a country, its resources of energy, the nature of its soil, its demography, its land area, etc.) and historical elements (national past, tradition, mentality, etc.), which obviously do not constitute two separate orders of 'factors', two distinct series of causes, but in their interaction upon one another combine to create the sum total of conditions to be taken into consideration, out of which men make history (yes, 'men' – Marx never uses any other word).

Consequently, a revolutionary policy will always come under a crossfire of accusations: cries of opportunism and empiricism from the left, and of maximalism and voluntarism from the right. Something should perhaps briefly be said here of the word 'realism'. In 1914, Lenin was accused of being unrealistic. This cannot be answered only by considering optical, stereoscopic metaphors which describe seeing what is close in relation to what is distant, and so on. The point is what one understands by the word 'reality', in other words, a whole conception of the world, a philosophy. The local politician, the professional realist, has a 'philosophy'. Unfortunately it is not a good philosophy: he is doomed to be the passive object, rather than the mover in history's changes. But if 'reality' is a process subject to certain laws, then it is right to move ahead, to be in advance of what is presented as reality at any given moment, so as to have some control over its transformation. Only by being 'ahead' of the present moment can one be fully 'inside' it. But that does not mean that it does not matter in which direction one goes 'ahead'; one's advance must be estimated from a true understanding of what it is that is to be overtaken. It is *this* moment that we must be 'ahead' of, and not some other; in other words, what we are essentially trying to do is to be part of the movement by which the present moment transcends itself to become the future. And this gives political foresight a special status: ultimately, foresight, or pre-vision, is simply a true vision of the present as it really is. When it came to foresight, Lenin, precisely because the theoretical axis of his practical action was the present moment, was far ahead of his comrades in the Party and even a number of people of his own stature: on his right was Bukharin; on his left Gramsci.

The unity of contraries makes it possible to understand the interdependence among the various aspects of their contradiction, and the various stages by which that contradiction develops. In open, declared antagonism, the mutual interaction of the forces involved, or of the aspects of the contradiction, becomes of decisive importance. Since each aspect provides the condition for the existence of the next, what affects one affects them all. A coup demands a counter-coup, action, reaction, and so on, until a decision is reached. A situation of open 'crisis' marks the point at which the forces in action discover the relationships by which they are likened and opposed, and the fact that it is only in those relationships that they exist. In normal circumstances those relationships remain concealed, neutralized into what looks merely passive co-existence. This mutual discovery reveals to each of the forces involved its own identity, by revealing to it the resistance and the nature of the antagonism of the opposing force. Each is then defined by its relationship to the other, and its discovery of that relationship. On both sides, the crisis awakens class consciousness; it brings distinctive features into sharp relief, brings new blood to the struggle, and stimulates recruitment from union and political class organizations, the promulgation of theories, and the circulation of newspapers. The more the disruptive forces advance, the more will the forces which support the older stability resist and re-form. (Was Stalin wrong to think that the class struggle grew fiercer after the proletariat had seized the power of the State? To judge from the experiences of several countries, it would seem that he was not. All the damage, the crimes and the evil resulted from his inability to distinguish among the various types of contradiction, and among the various ways of resolving them by the use of correct methods. A coup should be answered by a coup, an idea by another idea, a false thesis by a discussion, a political difference by political means rather than administrative or police measures. Furthermore, dialectic is not a blanket word: the 'afterwards' has its limits, the struggle changes form as it grows longer, the balance of forces tends to change to the advantage of the class in power, and so on. In short, though on paper he was a good dialectician, in practice Stalin, by the end of his life, had come to use deportation and assassination as a means to speculative metaphysics. To have mataphysics in power may well be physically dangerous to those being governed.)

Crisis and Revolutionary Situation: a Necessary Distinction

It is important here to note that though every revolutionary situation is inevitably a crisis situation, not every crisis situation is a revolutionary situation. Even though the antagonism may have come to the surface, and there has been a confrontation, and even though the power of the State may seem to have been brought seriously into question in that confrontation, it may still remain that the conditions are not ripe. One may not be able to risk throwing one's very existence into the balance, as a party or a class organization, with sufficient chance of success in making the leap that could win the day. Everything depends on the balance of forces, in other words, on knowing which one will be left out, which class will ally itself with which to create the weight of an *effective majority*. The capacity of the proletariat to intervene in the economic processes of production, through striking, for instance, gives it a special weight quite out of proportion to the numbers involved. But for how long, and in what political conditions? Ultimately, in a country like France, the exercise of political power depends on consolidating a powerful majority which would be capable of surviving a period of crisis; and such a force could only result from an alliance of the proletariat with the poor and slightly less poor farmers, and in the towns, with a large section of the petty bourgeoisie. Only the formation of such an alliance would make it possible for the revolutionary proletariat to control the exercise of power at the decisive, i.e. the political, level. It is not a very exciting prospect, and naturally tends to get forgotten in moments of springlike enthusiasm. The crisis does not make the revolution any more than the habit makes the monk. It is simply, in its organic form, its indispensable premise; by speaking of its organic form I mean a form affecting all the social classes in a given country – not one or two, but all at once – all the established power relationships, including that supremely organized power structure, the State.

Lenin said that: 'The fundamental law of revolutions, confirmed by all revolutions, especially the three Russian revolutions of the twentieth century, is this: for the exploited and oppressed masses to become aware that it is intolerable to continue living as they have lived, and to demand change, is not in itself enough to bring about a revolution. If there is to be a revolution, it must become impossible for the exploiters to live and rule as they have in the past. Revolution cannot happen *without a general national crisis.*' This idea is absolutely central and crucial in Lenin's strategy for seizing power. The national crisis itself is dependent on a situation of world crisis, combined with an international military conflict. And *only* in a situation of general national crisis and in no other situation – not a moment sooner or later, before or after – do the false problems of the 'normal course of things' disappear, or rather, do abstract contradictions find their practical solution; one such abstraction, for instance, is seeing the hypothetical active minority as being in opposition to the hypothetical electoral majority (not that either hypothesis is Leninist in the first place).

Only in the event of a crisis which brings everything to its extreme, when the exploited and dominated masses suddenly see the framework of their 'normal life' collapsing about them, their ideological illusions crumbling away, their legal representatives floundering about and unable to confront or dominate the new situation; only then can they rally in a practical, spontaneous, rapid way to the Party, or whatever other previously small organization they now see as representing their class interests. In three months, from July to September 1917, the Bolsheviks found their audience literally multiplied tenfold, as was clear from the elections to the Moscow municipal Douma which the Party leaders made their test case for deciding whether or not the uprising should take place.

Then, too, it is in a situation of general national crisis that the absolutely essential problem of the alliances of the proletariat, or the avant-garde class, can be favourably resolved. The problem is essential because only through the formation of a new class alliance can the minority avant-garde class be converted into an effective majority. And the solution will be favourable to the extent that the avant-garde succeeds in proving that it does really represent what Engels calls 'the national class', the only class whose leadership would in future be capable of handling the defence of the whole nation's interests. In China, the turning-point of 1937, of the 'United Anti-Japanese Front', marked the date from which it became clear to the mass of the Chinese people that the preservation of their national independence was organic-ally bound up with the victory of the Communist Party and the People's Army of Liberation. And it was no mere chance that the Chinese Party then centred on Yenan suddenly increased its membership tenfold and was able to extend the zones of libera-tion, and consolidate itself as a Party, while at the same time achieving the policy of the alliance of the 'four classes' which had been outlined in the heat of the fight for the New Democracy.

A Parenthesis on the Problem of Alliances

On this capital problem there is much to be learnt from the works of Mao, though they are curiously little used by most of his European disciples. Briefly in the context of a dualism of categories at the strategic level (of revolution versus counter-revolution, socialism versus imperialism, East versus West) at which we can recognize the rhythm in the 'turning-points', and note the up-heavals in the balance of power,[1] as well as tracing the political and ideological demarcation lines (the 'goodies' and 'baddies') – in that context there is room for a subtle, moment-by-moment pluralism in the distinction among classes and levels of society at the tactical level. In analysing the class structure among country people, for instance, we distinguish four basic levels, and even within the first, the rich farmer class, there are those of the old school and those of the new; and so on. In towns we have to distinguish the monopolist *comprador* bourgeoisie, the national bourgeoisie and the petty bourgeoisie. All this is involved in determining the policy of *alliances* at any given time, depending on the aims in view. The correctness of a line may be judged by the alliances on which it rests. The *gauchiste* errors of 1931–4 alien-ated the middle peasants. During the alliance with the Kuomin-tang, the scope for making other alliances was reduced, since there was no agrarian reform, but only a reduction in interest rates and farm rents and things of that kind. Then there was the phase of the 'New Democracy', with the four classes, and so on.

In other words, there are several distinct 'classes' within each class of Chinese society, and every political period brings different alliances of forces into play. But in essence, the basic rhythm, the basic reasoning, is not dualist but *ternary*. And while every situation, every historical junction must be grasped as a whole, it must also be analysed in terms of the numbers two and three: the strategic two, the tactical three. It is here that we find the fundamental error of *gauchisme*: it sees the two so clearly as to be blind to the three. For if there are only two camps: there is a struggle between two entities – labour and capital, and two classes – bourgeoisie and proletariat, but nothing between the two. True, there *are* only two camps, but there are three forces, and if the revolutionary camp is to win the day, it must of necessity be extended to include the pivotal forces, those upon whom victory

1. Mao Tse-tung, *The Present Situation and Our Tasks*, I, 1947, in Selected Works, published by the Foreign Languages Press, Peking.

or defeat hinges – it may be the peasants, it may be the petty bourgeoisie, it may be both. *Gauchisme* – dualist and Manichean – is incapable of achieving a successful policy of alliances. The basis for the right policy is this: 'To develop progressive forces, to win over the intermediate forces, and to isolate the forces of the extremists.'[1]

In the event, isolating the enemy and winning over the moderates becomes a single operation, because both are achieved by depriving the enemy of his possible allies. And the three terms are really only one, since the moderates, if they are not won over by us will be won over by the enemy, who will then achieve a majority and take from the progressive forces all possibility of developing further.

Here is a useful description of the masses in general: 'The masses consist of a minority who are active, a majority who are undecided, and a minority who are passive. We must develop the first in order to attract the second and thus neutralize the third.'

In this sense, at the political level the class struggle always appears as a 'three-sided duel', a duel between two parties for the conquest of the third, and consequent isolation of the opponent.

The history of revolutions in France, both the successes and the failures, from 1789 to 1968, should be written schematically along these lines. In each case the intermediary forces involved, the forces in dispute, should be identified – those forces whose support or lack of it has spelt victory or failure. In 1789, the peasants of The Great Fear gave their support. In 1848, the peasants were alienated from the first by Garnier-Pagès' forty-five centimes tax, and refused their support. And then in May 1968 came the upheaval in the urban 'middle classes', crystallized by de Gaulle's speech on the thirtieth of May.

But not every 'general national crisis', however great its disruptive effect on society may seem to be, necessarily provides *all* the conditions that will ensure a victorious revolutionary breakthrough. As the Leninist adage has it, 'Everything depends on the conditions and circumstances'; and this is not the place to go into

1. *The Present Situation and Our Tasks*, VII.

all the conditions and circumstances of the May crisis. We must recognize what distinguishes a crisis situation from a revolutionary one. In the former, the class in power can always find some way round, some other solution to preserve the *status quo*, some central, in-between path that misses the sharp turn; they may even steer into the turn themselves if that is the only way of holding on to their control – but in any case they will find some subterfuge to get them out of making a clear-cut choice. In the latter, there can be no recourse to a compromise solution, no superficial rearrangement of the old balance, but only total defeat or total victory for one of the two opposing sides in the struggle.

'We have no Treaty with victory, but only with the battle'

A revolutionary situation does not mean a situation in which revolution is like a ripe fruit which will fall easily into our hand if we shake or twist the branch. It is merely a situation in which one can no longer remain neutral, in which one must face up to the alternatives: revolution or counter-revolution; a situation in which the ruling class or classes cannot return to the old order in which the majority of those ruled were able to forget that they were being dominated, and therefore accept it. Either the ruling class must become openly dominant, abandoning all subterfuges, all palliatives, or they must be openly overcome. It is a situation in which there is no place for equivocation or compromise: the two camps are utterly distinct. Having come to the fork in the road, you must go either left or right, because the road you were on stops there. It must be either Lenin or Kornilov, but it absolutely cannot be Kerensky, because Kerensky is equivalent to Kornilov – which is why the crisis had to be decided one way or the other after July and the failure of Kornilov's provisional putsch. In a matter of months, the crisis shifted the centre of gravity of the Kerensky government towards the monarchist counter-revolution. There could be no intermediate position.

The special dynamic of any revolutionary situation lies in the fact that third parties have to settle for one camp or the other; the duel becomes *directly strategic* because the alternatives are presented in their extreme form. A situation may be said to be revolutionary not because revolution has become inevitable: it is not, will not be, and never has been inevitable at any time in history. A situation is revolutionary from the moment when it becomes inevitable that if there is not a revolution now, then there will be a counter-revolution tomorrow, and vice versa; either dictatorship by the people or dictatorship by the Armed Forces, either socialism or fascism, either liberation or slavery. (Consider Italy from 1920 to 1923, the Weimar Republic, Santo Domingo in 1965, Bolivia in 1964, Vietnam, Indonesia, and so on.) Such historical and local situations, though obviously no one is identical with any other, have in common, both in the past and the present, not the inevitability of revolution, but the inevitability of choosing between revolution and counter-revolution, independence and submission. The spontaneity of history can only lead us to such crossroads of crisis, when the last word must be said by 'politics' – in fact by struggle in general, political, military and ideological, or in other words the tendency of that struggle. One cannot therefore speak of revolutionary spontaneity, for always, sooner or later, but inevitably, there will be a general crisis which forces a 'decision'.

It is wise to remember here that a revolutionary situation can and also must be considered as a counter-revolutionary situation, if one is to be in any kind of control of its results. And the effect of the dialectical development of things is that the closer an oppressed class gets to the power of the State, the harder it is for its representatives to take hold of it. In the area of practical tactics, clear-sighted leaders must act as though victory is all the more distant for being so close. One cannot, for instance, gather into one united front the mass of people in an attempt to transform the conditions in which they live, without provoking a corresponding gathering of the forces of reaction – which will probably respond faster, and be better armed since they own the

State machine. It is crazy to imagine one without the other, or to plan one's action without taking into account the reaction. This may sound like the merest banality, yet it is all too often forgotten, with the following disastrous results:

– Surprise, confusion and bitterness over what are thought to be 'unjust', 'illogical', even 'incomprehensible' reverses, reverses which can only be understood in terms of the action of 'traitors', 'Judases', 'incompetents', etc. We see it in the newspapers: 'Never had there been so many of us in the streets, never had there been such widespread mobilization – ten million strikers, revolutionaries, Bolsheviks, people who really were ready for anything . . . and then, suddenly, from one day to the next, the balloon went down, everybody vanished, and the enemy held all the cards . . . ' Or, more seriously, consider how fascism in Italy and Germany ran parallel to the development of socialism in those countries. A succession of plus signs does not guarantee a positive result. Politics is algebra, not arithmetic, and a crisis is like an algebraic problem.

– Sad sighs, and bitter reproaches from the reformists at every evidence of extremism; these people basically believe that contradictions are resolved not by becoming sharper or fiercer, but by fading gently away to a point of extinction. They believe that for a contradiction to disappear is the same as for it to be resolved. Such dialectical para-logic is what leads to comments of this kind: 'The riots in the American ghettos will get Nixon elected; they will win votes for Wallace. If the Blacks were more prudent, if the extremist students were wiser, we might have had a nice Democrat for president, a fine man we could all admire.' (Not that anyone quite admits the full extent of his feelings. You have to read between the lines.) During the period of the great illusions of the international workers' movement (1958–65), when people talked in terms of 'cosmic' victories, of communism in twenty years, national bourgeoisies, a new type of democrat, Sukharno, Nkrumah, etc., this was the fundamental reasoning which underlay the so-called struggle for peace. In the name of such reasoning, the Vietnamese were asked to lessen their resistance so as not to jeopardize world peace. The text might have run like this: 'These dangerous centres of international tension, which do not merely endanger peace while contributing nothing to improving the lot of ordinary people, actually do them harm by providing a pretext for imperialism to intervene . . . ', and so on.

Now in these common reactions there are two quite distinct elements. One is perfectly justifiable. It involves an anxiety to avoid the kind of provocations, adventurist and premature actions, which may jeopardize the future, precisely because the period in which class, national or international oppositions develop is not the 'cumulative interiorization' of explosive elements, but a delicate network of interwoven strategic points. It is impossible to provoke or improvise crisis situations artificially; every country, every locality has its own special historical time, its own pace, its speed of development. But this element is unfortunately overlaid by, or used as a pretext for a cheap evolutionism: it is assumed that there is a *naturally* 'progressive' advance in the nature of things, continuous, regular, cumulative and measured, which will become evident when the time is ripe, following the inevitable dialectic of history, having on its way got rid of all that was bad in the old order of things. Some such concept shows clearly through the commentaries, drawing strength from passing revolutionary setbacks, as though the road to success were not strewn throughout history with sacrifices and defeats. In the abstract, any attempt to break with the imperialist *status quo* could be accused of being provocative, for it is bound to provoke a reaction from the enemy. Only an analysis of actual local conditions makes it possible to say whether or not the 'provocation' is good, healthy and progressive, or useless and inopportune. In the nature of the case, reformists do not take great risks. They know very well that from an objective, statistical point of view, any revolutionary movement is courting failure at every moment. They can easily, then, condemn it in advance, or else ignore the whole thing with silence that speaks louder than words. In the history of revolutions everyone knows that success is the exception rather than the rule. But one exception is enough to turn a whole era upside down and remodel history completely; a link may give at one end of the world, and the far-off end of the chain will quiver at the other. (Which is why what may happen tomorrow in some South American Macondo, though Macondo itself is of no importance as compared with Paris or Tokyo, might have quite unforeseeable effects on events in Paris or Toyko in the future.)

The Two Abstractions, or Brothers Who Are Enemies

Metaphysics in the field of history: it has a single root, but two faces. The root is the consideration of forces in themselves, independent of the connection with one another. It is the connection which is the concrete reality in every situation; and the changes in that connection determine how one 'present moment' turns into the next. 'Present moment' is a political term, for it is at the level of the political arm of an economic-cum-social formation that the opposing forces enter fully into relationship with one another, and that what Lenin called 'the combined action of social forces' takes place. It is therefore at the political level that a social formation becomes a reality, and the result of that 'realization' is the present moment which constitutes the object of all effective political action. In a crisis situation, the present moment tends to come very close to being definable as the 'moment when two forces join'. Thus it is more than ever necessary to consider the product of the two, and to consider them both in and through their product – in other words, not to make the mistake of a unilateral abstraction. To envisage a situation from all its aspects means to consider the interdependence of those aspects; to grasp the unity of the situation as something that is a result, a product, means treating it dialectically. There are two ways of avoiding the dialectical task, two ways of bringing it back to metaphysics, one on the right, the other on the left.

Marx speaks of the first in the *Manifesto*: 'The socialistic bourgeois want all the advantages of modern social conditions without the struggles and dangers necessarily resulting therefrom. They desire the existing state of society minus its revolutionary and disintegrating elements. They wish for a bourgeoisie without a proletariat.' It fell to Lenin to defend himself against the second, the other form of metaphysical socialism which he called *gauchisme*. The *gauchistes* also want the conditions of modern life and society without the alliances and the relative stability which must flow from them. They want society as it is, but purged of the elements which keep it in being and tend to restore its unity. They want the proletariat without the bourgeoisie. They do not understand the opposition and the solidarity of opposites, and they make it impossible to derive any fruit from the relationship between the two by shutting their eyes to its existence.

Leftist abstraction is a kind of mirror-image of the opportunist abstraction of the right. Such unreal disputes are real dramas of history, because they actually spill over into the arena where the fighting takes place, as in Europe today for instance. The two abstractions foster and justify each other: the vicious circle can be an objective effect of the dialectic 'in things themselves'. One could produce quite a list of the unreal disputes which make Europe, whether capitalist or socialist, East or West, so fertile a ground for sterile outgrowths – starting with the dispute which contrasts and links the two Europes as they are at present. (At the theoretical level, for instance, there is the debate between eclectic humanism and rigorist scientism, between unification and separation, based on the motion that one deviation can only be corrected by a deviation in the opposite direction. It then becomes a matter not of abstractly criticizing the terms at issue, but of understanding the historical conditions which have turned such false alternatives into the concrete, necessary, and at present inevitable horizon of the development of dialectical materialism, which is itself subject to the laws of the struggle of opposites, of uneven development, of opinions being turned upside down to adapt to crises, and so on. To understand historical conditions in this case includes understanding the data of theoretical history, but not only them, for in the final analysis they are merely an abstract reflection of the concrete history of the European class struggle since the war.)

These two abstractions feed upon one another. Whatever political form they may take, whatever the circumstances in which they exist, as tendencies or 'structures of the ideological consciousness', they indicate a rhetorical, indefinitely recurring, utterly lifeless opposition. To describe them faithfully in their own terms, one might give an *abstract* account, retaining only the essential features. The first tendency abstracts from objectively existing conditions; the second from the movement to break through those conditions. But there is no 'first', no 'second' – since each is a spontaneous reaction to the other, it is a chicken-and-egg relationship.

A political line is revolutionary when it adopts the means to break through 'previously existing conditions' by basing itself upon them, *starting* from them – but doing so in order to achieve an objective which is never wholly implicit *in* them, an objective that lies beyond. It is this contradictory effort which unites the theoretical aspect with the practical, a formal contradiction which is resolved in action, but admits of no final, once-for-all solution, because it is no sooner resolved than it presents itself again in a different and unexpected form. Its solution can only be a constant movement of criticism and self-criticism relating both to the centre and the periphery of the revolutionary party: how can one work one's way into the mechanics of capitalist society without being absorbed by it? How can one be both inside and out, here and beyond? How can a party become a party of the masses while still fulfilling its function as vanguard? How can one manage to defend bourgeois democracy against itself; how, in the daily ideological and political struggle, continue to oppose one's own democratic–liberal principles to bourgeois practice, and at the same time transcend, and thus in a sense deny, those principles? How can one be committed to the hilt in the wage-claims struggle without becoming bogged down in trade-unionism?

Rosa Luxemburg saw this problem very clearly; what is odd is that she failed to see the aspect of it which was to prove so catastrophic in 1914 – the problem of reconciling the national situation with proletarian internationalism – despite all the vague reassurances of Jaurès. Those are the forms in which the contradiction appears simultaneously at a given moment. In fact, as it works out in time, during a period of historical activity, it is resolved through an interaction between the breaking-point and the point at which cohesion is restored, whether in the Party, in society as a whole, or in a nation's history. To take an example of this, the contradiction might appear in these terms, still in the form of a problem, a 'how', the problem of resolution: how to become a part of the national continuity (of history or of feeling) so as to force a revolutionary break – during the time of a power struggle? The problem then becomes: how, starting from the break, the overthrow of the old unity, to draw back together the threads of national continuity (rejecting the *Proletkults*, restoration of the old values of patriotism, education in the culture and language of the past, and so on)?

In proletarian or student or any other form, and in the various periods in which *gauchisme* has been forced into appearing as a punishment, or perhaps expiation, for the sin of opportunism, it tends to exalt the end ultimately in view – the break – as against its roots in the earth, in the mass of the people, in popular ideology and national history. This is an important point. The movement whereby a group of militants pull themselves clear of the historical muddles of opportunism is bound to demand a strong act of will, instead of continuing to work passively within the normal course of events, they are summoning up their forces to act as agents. By that very fact, they tend to skip the usual processes of beginnings, and create for themselves a present without any past, since what is past cannot be changed. Now the people, the masses – though these terms can become the basis for a metaphysical or rhetorical discussion – only appear in the concrete reality of history as strands woven into the fabric of national traditions. The nation itself, a community of language, of territory and of outlook (to adopt the restricted but accurate definition given by Stalin) constitutes the evident, tangible form of tradition;

and here I use 'tradition' to mean the continuous movement of the past into the present, the mutual interaction of the two. The nation's form of existence in history demonstrates the presence of the past, and indeed the presence of nature (which already exists) in history (which is still coming into being) and of the conditions for the genesis of a social structure in its more developed state. The fact that political action, even proletarian internationalism, can only exist actively in the framework of national structures, with all their many limitations, geographical, historical, mental, religious, linguistic, and so on, constantly recalls us to that dialectical truth so bitter to the utopias of voluntarists, the truth that though we are always involved with historical nature, we are never dealing solely with natural history. For 'nature' is not just what lets itself be determined by our will, but also what determines our will. In this sense, in admitting that what we perhaps somewhat loosely lump together under the title of '*gauchisme*' involves an exaltation of the voluntarist element, it is of the essence of that tendency to have a short memory, whether individually or politically: to us the past belongs to 'nature'.

But it is important to see just how healthy and normal is this form of amnesia. It is an almost instinctive and spontaneous defence reaction of youth against old age, of the movement of life against the opportunist paralysis of our institutional structures, our museum-keepers and the revolutionary dogmas of the past. Though note that this reaction must in its turn be transcended and left behind, or it too will become its own form of paralysis. It is a reaction against those to whom memory and ' experience ' dictate inactivity and a repetition of past patterns, who are careful never to make a speech without due preparation, so that it may have its full quota of quotations, clichés and references to the past, against those who spend their lives commemorating the giants of old who provide them with their alibis. There is no revolutionary politician who has not got a tradition to fall back on, the inextricably interwoven tradition of a class and a country; in this sense no wholehearted communist need apologize for being a man of tradition. Indeed he is the agent of tradition, he is the man who represents in the present day the historical interests of his country and his class. A revolutionary must be deeply soaked in the history of his own people, and indeed that of all mankind. A French revolutionary must not only know about 1789, but about the crusades and Clovis; a Vietnamese must have studied the great battles against the Mongols. But to any revolutionary, tradition is in itself something practical, something that must be brought to bear on the activities of the present. It is not something to close in on itself, not a dead weight or a devotion to the 'good old days'; otherwise there can be no interaction, the past will not be the life-giving transfusion of blood it should be to the present. Our notion of tradition will endanger or even destroy some traditions, just as our notion of the nation leads us on to internationalism. We certainly start from that, but only in order to proceed beyond it; in this way there is nothing abstract about our internationalism, because it is based on the concrete reality of what a nation is, and then rather than turning it into an abstraction, subsumes it into what is a wider reality.

Gauchisme demands a 'rupture', without knowing of what; it is in a void, nowhere and everywhere. The total break of the revolution ends up by presenting itself as an absolute; the slogan becomes an exhortation to understanding; the work of organization is replaced by moral duty. An undifferentiated protest comes to apply equally to everything, unvarying from one country, one set of circumstances, one social situation to the next.

Right-wing opportunism delays the moment of the break indefinitely, It never fails to point out how inopportune this particular moment is, and to ridicule or argue away what look like signs that the time is ripe. It talks of the gains achieved by continuity and tradition, which generally take the forms of fidelity to the programme or resolutions of previous congresses, relating to a situation that no longer exists, these it contrasts with the way in which the demand for rupture depends on unreliable circumstances, on abandoning definite gains and, in the short term at least, risking the loss of everything. So deeply is it implicated in the bourgeois world that instead of using the world as it exists now as a basis for speeding up that world's dissolution, that world is able to use it as a prop for its own survival. For, thanks to this particular 'opposition' which makes periodic reforms unachievable, that world manages to make minor modifications which do not change its nature, manages to change without being overthrown. Even the crises which rock bourgeois society thus end up by becoming stabilizing factors for the ruling class.

Ideological Digression on Trotskyism (as the Construct of an Uneasy Conscience)

Since we seem to have got into metaphysics, we might as well stay there for a while, in company with that most sympathetic of all revolutionary metaphysics which burst fully armed from the unjustly battered head of that fascinating man, Trotsky, the greatest socialist writer after Marx himself. We will leave aside all theoretical considerations of Trotskyism as a theory. In his time, the time when it was the moving force behind the left opposition, Gramsci summarized in a few words the profound rejection of opportunism which even then set him at loggerheads with the times: Trotsky – a strategist of attack in a period of defence and withdrawal enforced by the balance of forces from 1923 onwards. If one burrows beneath the theoretical, one may go further: could it be that non-opportunism is the permanent and essential mark of Trotskyism, in a sense its whole *raison d'être*, whether as the political representation of a state of awareness, or as an ahistorical *Weltanschauung* leading to, or supported by an ancient and unchanging religion of suffering? Why is two minutes' conversation enough to show one 'the Trotskyist' in a stranger?

There is the vocabulary of course, or what passes for one, the three or four basic terms, bureaucracy, Thermidor, self-management, etc. More, there is a tone of voice, with that certain sardonic, or mocking, or unhappy grating quality about it, a kind of bitterness or frustration. The Trotskyist, permanently in opposition, even within his own organizations, always between two dissident groups, seems to tend naturally to resentment. He is betrayed and deceived; he is not going to let it happen again, either to himself or the proletariat, whose Quisling leaders will soon be unmasked; his most intelligent associates will join the Fourth International. His tone indicates a certain attitude to the world, a certain structuring of experience. Here is a noble soul bewailing the way things have gone, been perverted, the truth distorted, the good rejected. The Bureaucracy is a ten-thousand-headed monster, and it is all the Bureaucracy's evil doing.

Like so many fine souls, the Trotskyist bewails an evil he could not do without, an evil which in the end his wails serve to support. Since every incarnation of the socialist revolution in history is contaminated at source, there can be nothing wrong in casting doubt on it all – it is merely a precaution, and *a priori* a valid one. All this is very like the philosophical Judaism defined by the young Hegel in *The Origin and Destiny of Christianity*. One could say of Trotskyism, as of Abraham, that ' its separation from any destiny is just what its highest destiny is '. The worker-cum-peasant government and the proletariat are two abstract universals which can never change, which will inevitably dry up in the bitterness of accusation, because they can never link up with the actual fact of *this* socialist government, *this* proletariat here and now. There can be no reconciliation with the Law. The ideal must always transcend what is actually being done. Anything that actually happens is guilty for compromising with reality. Trotskyism itself, all-knowing and all-critical (and here I mean that point of pure idealism at which the fragmented sections of the Fourth International are linked), transcends any responsibility in the concrete; it is not answerable to any state, any people, any revolution actually going on. This is not just by ill-luck or accident, but a need, almost a duty, of its nature. Its nature is to defeat nature, to withdraw from anything that might be positive, to act forever the negative role of the professional explosives man borrowed from Hegel. Only something that can be seen as negative can it consider respectable: in every case one must learn to recognize the dividing line between the suspect and the pure.

In Vietnam the struggle is wonderfully pure, but they are careful not to look too closely at its political content – the programme of the NLF, the political alliances, the nature of North Vietnam and its socialist régime, all subjects on which 'there are reservations to be made'. The same is true of the relationship of Cuba with Che, or rather of the ahistorical caricature they have, all unwittingly and with the best intentions made of it. Unfortunately, the day will come when power is achieved, when the negative will come to mean something definite. It must always be *a* power, *a* state, *a* nation. Any policy is positive, therefore natural, therefore suspect; it will be related to a geographical situation, a national history, a particular culture, a section of civilization. This content is a blot on the abstract and universal; it is a fact, a destiny, like the fact that a certain socialist state may not have enough natural resources of energy (coal, oil, watercourses), may be thousands of miles away from its nearest friendly neighbour, may be involved by its past as a single-crop country in foreign trade and world markets, and so on. All these are *facts*, which do not admit of the possibility of adopting whatever policy one might prefer at any time, which give the policy that *has* been chosen its possibility of success – but which also enable the metaphysicians to rush into making the irresponsible accusation of 'opportunism', of which only they are the judges.

To Trotskyists and other metaphysicians there are no pure socialist states, if only because the only states that merit the name of socialist are national states, and there are reservations to be made about them all. How successful have been the Trotskyist attempts at historical 'incarnations' – the MNR's Bolivia, Ben Bella's Algeria, Guatemala? Ultimately Trotskyism must also fail to become embodied in the youth of France. Certainly there was an empty place, ideologically unoccupied, ready for the taking. But it will never be able to occupy that place fully, as it really is; not merely because there will be other movements outside it to prevent it, but because it will be prevented from within as well. It is not a tactical ruse for the old faithfuls of the Fourth International to retreat before the young; that retreat, to quote

Hegel again, is the non-position of Abraham as a nomad, having no land, no world, no neighbours of his own, feeding his flocks where he could and then moving on. The conscience of the Trotskyist excludes everything; and everyone else excludes him. He will no more dispense himself from his exile than he will forgive others for exiling him. The fragmentation which is his natural element, from which he suffers but which he also enjoys, is actually inside himself. There is no such thing as a happy Trotskyist. His misfortunes and failures justify and confirm him in his final distaste for 'bureaucracies'. By the fact that he rejects every concrete embodiment of socialism from the centre of his theoretical circle of pure forms, he is actually expelling himself from the reality of history. The wheel always comes full circle: the Trotskyist is always right.

What a posthumous fate for so admirable a man as Trotsky! This infinitely adaptable ideology which he might perhaps have disowned and which certainly could not have been his: this thing which he certainly would not have wanted to be, but which has finally become him. One may call it his fate, just as it is the fate of political terminology to awaken by such reflections as this certain related ideas that are suspect – connected with the 'wooden language'[1] and the sinister Stalinist repressions – which still remain alive in this area. Such compulsive anathemas belong to the past. The tremendous achievement of the revolution now going on in Latin America is to have swept away all these prejudices inherited from Europe, and to that extent to have 'desectarianized' us; to have taught us to distinguish the importance of militants as people, all with the same rights and duties in relation to the common task, which all confront together, from each one's links with the classical ideologies. One must have unlimited respect and admiration for a Hugo Blanco, for Cesar Lora, for Gonzales Moscoso, and all the nameless victims of the Bolivian mines, all of whom might be lumped together as 'Trotskyists'.

1. This is a modern communist argot term for a language made up wholly of formulae and jargon, lacking any resonance. It was coined especially to describe the Stalinist period.

The Twofold Role of Politico-Social Crises in Capitalist Society

In the history of advanced capitalist societies there are 'bilateral' examples – crises in which two strands are interwoven. In this connection we may recall the anticipation in the *Manifesto*: 'The bourgeoisie cannot exist without constantly revolutionizing the instruments of production, and thereby the relations of production, and with them the whole relations of society. Conservation of the old modes of production in unaltered form was, on the contrary, the first condition of existence for all earlier industrial classes. Constant revolutionizing of production, uninterrupted disturbance of all social conditions, everlasting uncertainty and agitation distinguish the bourgeois epoch from all earlier ones.' The bourgeoisie thus of its nature develops by way of a series of crises. The capitalist mode of production is revolutionary in that it involves and produces incessant technical changes in the production system, accompanied by economic, ideological and political crises. To assume that such upheavals herald the end of the system is dangerously naïve. From one point of view, that is precisely how capitalism manifests its vitality, the growth of its productive forces, and, politically, its capacity for reshuffling the cards, creating new class alliances. This is quite obvious in imperialist wars, those perfected and multilateral forms of 'the general crisis in the imperialist system', which have in fact simply acted as a fresh stimulus to its productive forces (in the United States especially), or provided it with the occasion for a new start, a renewal of economic growth by liquidating the remnants of feudalism or outworn production systems (as in Germany and Japan).

In other words, capitalism is well able to turn its own crises to good effect, and actually draw new strength from them. One may even measure the vitality of a bourgeois society by its capacity to welcome or absorb its own crises, its internal dissensions, the forces that would otherwise split it apart. Portugal simply ignores crises, and the *escudo* remains strong; Portuguese stability is the symptom of economic and political stagnation, of the extreme weakness of its capitalist development and the ideological inconsistency of its ruling class. This stagnation is the symptom of a far more incurable sickness than the succession of blows that have shaken French and Italian society. On the other hand, the capitalist semi-colonies of Latin America live in a state of permanent crisis, but cannot manage to use it to stimulate a genuine bourgeois development. The Latin American bourgeoisies are incapable of making capital out of their political and economic crises; their power as rulers over the rest of their society is so frail and unsteady that they are forced to solve their crises by simply suppressing them, by the physical repression of police measures. A constant recourse to sheer force is symptomatic of intense weakness in the ruling class. Every strike, every demonstration, every attack, however minor, on its power is disallowed in the institutional system, and so becomes pushed into a position of 'subversion', with force as its only weapon against brute force. The inability of the ruling class to cope with crises is expressed by its lack of political flexibility, by that inertia rocked by the incoherent spasms and convulsions of reaction which occur regularly in Latin America. Just as it has been unable to advance in any organic and independent way to an accumulation of capital, so too the ruling class, the pseudo-bourgeoisie, manifests its inability to move forward politically, to build up any flexible political time. The successions of political régimes, the everlasting *coups d'état*, the upheavals and about-turns of the various *caudillos*, are all so many caricatures of the whole bourgeois instability, of a movement which is unceasing but entirely without depth. In such a situation, the permanent political crisis becomes the symptom of economic and social stagnation, the expression of a non-dialectical movement of time.

If one goes on to consider a ruling class whose domination goes back a long time, a genuinely bourgeois society like the French, one can recognize its capacity for converting internal oppositions into a force for renewal (though only, of course, relatively speaking, since the total structure remains unchanged); the social adversary being a party to the process, whether willingly or not. Hence the incontestable audacity, the freedom of mind, and general receptiveness of the French bourgeoisie which to, say, the bourgeoisie of Bolivia is so incomprehensible as to be almost scandalous. The very word 'bourgeois' is painfully inadequate, if you think that France and Bolivia today, both societies 'in theory' belonging to the same side in the international class struggle, both in the 'bourgeois camp', are totally unsusceptible to any comparative quantitative evaluation (as more or less developed, more or less 'feudal', etc.). They are two worlds of social domination utterly different in kind, two planets far distant from each other in both time and space. In Bolivia, for instance, *Le Figaro* is a subversive newspaper which would not be allowed into the country!

It is this social and historical capacity to absorb and to recuperate, that enables the bourgeoisie to see its unity in terms of a movement, and to turn every split into something inevitable and ultimately helpful to its own cohesion. In Italy, for example, the arrival with Cavour of the bourgeois society, and the creation of a whole new mentality inside the old are brilliantly depicted by Lampedusa in *The Leopard*, in the rupture between the father and son, the feudal lord faced with his own fear of the careful adventurer, who conceives of audacity as the surest way of preserving the patriarchal interests, and permits the red shirt of Garibaldi up to a certain point. 'One must change things so that they will not change.' This capacity enables it to force its opponents to fight on its own home ground (ideological, institutional, electoral). In France a respect for legality is objectively a republican tradition, historically left-wing and Jacobin (as against the factionalists of La Vendée, Boulanger, etc.), yet it now functions under the effective control of the Right.

It is not a matter of falling into a kind of inversely unilateral position, but of trying to give back to the 'crises' of bourgeois society their historical ambivalence. One must stress the notion that in the last analysis, the crises peculiar to capitalist development are not necessarily what is at issue, for a crisis may be turned to good or bad account, rightly or wrongly understood. In this context, a crisis is not of itself like the preview of a play, or, rather, it is a preview *also* for those who have no interest in whether the première itself ever takes place. It serves as a warning to both sides, both of which, perhaps one more than the other, can make use of those of its effects, draw from it those lessons, which best serve their purpose. The determining factor remains the political and theoretical treatment of the crisis itself, and of society as affected by the crisis. What may herald the end of this social structure in its present form may also from another standpoint be what enables it to survive. The last word lies with the doctors, that is those politically in charge. Of course one can sagely declare that it will certainly die some day, that there is a *law* of succession for social structures, that capitalism 'gives birth to its own negation with the inevitability of any other natural metamorphosis'. There will come a time when we have seriously to question the type of inevitability which is at work in the general historical process, and whether the same one is at work in the same way in the different stages of social development, the same in the primitive community as in monopoly capitalism.

Let us say for now that medicine would not have developed far, and mankind still less, if we had clung since the time of Hippocrates to that undeniable, alarmingly abstract and negative, and, if pushed to its furthest point, terrifying certainty that every living organism is destined by nature to die; and that if one cannot cure death, there is little point in giving a few extra years of life to someone who is ill. Little point to whom? And in terms of what 'higher interests'?

A crisis of government, a politico-social crisis, in this context, acts both as a revelation, disclosing structures, and yet also as a veil, an ideological smokescreen. It reveals the presence of contradictions – as for instance between the socialization of capitalist production and the private appropriation of profit – and the objective basis for the continuance of the class struggle, thus giving the lie to the dominant ideology. But it also re-forms that ideology, showing it which are the most sensitive points in the system of institutions, such as the university, in which a series of unresolved contradictions may be merging together so dangerously as to be approaching crisis point, demographic growth, worn-out equipment, teaching quite inadequate to the demands of production, lack of outlets, a crisis in the prevailing ideology, and so on. In such a situation a crisis may for a time serve to save the diseased organ by drawing the ruling class's attention to it in time. A fever indicates that there is a sickness, but it also makes it possible to localize it, to identify it, to *isolate* the worst affected organ, and to bring to bear whatever medication may be needed. A crisis, like a fever, is both a bad sign and a useful signal to the ruling class. Far better to have a recognized infection, a gaping wound, than a generalized cancer eating away inside which is not diagnosed because it presents no external symptoms.

I choose these medical metaphors with more seriousness than might at first appear. Bourgeois democracy has one great advantage over a bureaucratized socialism, in being able to apply all forms of preventive medicine as indicated by the thermometers of election results, the periodic X-rays made of the socio-political body, opinion polls, the thermostat of the opposition, the whole gamut of permissible and tolerable conflicts (economic strikes, political campaigns, ideological attacks), whereby a dominant class manages to preserve a precarious balance by making its own adjustments, defending its most vital points, and stopping up the most serious breaches (in 1968 it was the remarkable clinician Edgar Fauré who closed the university breach). What happened in 1936 represented a great victory for the working class, but it was not a victory that involved a major defeat for the upper middle class. Politically it was short. Socially, its fundamental gains remained, but not only did they have constantly to be defended, or re-won, from another point of view they provided the exploitation relationship with a new balance, a new way of working. Obviously the memory of any great crisis will be a stimulus. It highlights a tradition of struggle, strengthens class consciousness, reveals the enemy's weakness and the immense possibilities of the masses if they unite, and thus underlines the need for unity, and so on. But in ideological memory, the myth of the crisis as it develops contains a certain opiate element. The lyrical evocation, the conventionalized memory, these conceal the fact that the crisis was ultimately brought under control by the system, and used by it, and may even have served the political or economic objective of the system; the system itself thus continued to function as before. The myth works as an evasion phantasy, an ideal consolation; though it can mobilize, it can also paralyse the present-day movement by continuing to relate it to a *pattern*, a *norm* that is past. It then creates its own group of 'old soldiers', former fighters now armed with the principle of authority ('You weren't there in '36,' 'You weren't there in '45', 'You weren't around in May, Comrade, so just shut up, you don't know what you're talking about'); they are the proletarian equivalents of the We-didn't-see-*you*-at-Verdun-young-man type of retired soldier.

Briefly, June 1936 and May 1968 can be considered as issues still in dispute, still hanging in suspense, while at the same time they also constitute determining moments in the decision process.

A crisis may be defined as 'a decisive and dangerous moment in the evolution of things'. One must not let oneself get carried away by the mystique of the crisis, close as it is to the various mystiques of violence as an abstract synonym for revolution, and of apocalyptic fantasies. Nor should one envisage social evolution as something that goes in a straight line, a series of 'successive conquests', 'progressive stages', in which there are no crossroads, none of those side-turnings along which one may have occasion to go and thus re-examine the whole direction of the course one is planning (the road to socialism for instance), or even the victories one may already have won. That is another kind of mystique, a pseudo-rationalist one. Nor must one let oneself be misled by the old reverence for suffering (individual or social) as a means to purification and redemption, 'civil society' thereby being redeemed from its 'sins' – failure of awareness, mediocrity, complicity in the civil war. But in history one has to pay for one's insensitivity to pain with many more and worse pains in the end. When, just before October, Lenin thought in terms of a painless transition to socialism, he had in mind only a minimal chance that, though it could be seized at once, could at the most do no more than delay the trial of force with the warring imperial countries who were allied to the reactionary elements inside the country. One must recognize what Czechoslovakia and indeed the other People's Democracies have paid and have yet to pay for the fact of having a socialism to which they themselves had not given birth, which was never fully their own but always remained the 'child from next-door', an object of diplomatic negotiations and bargaining.

It is no mere chance that biological and organic metaphors recur so systematically in the writings of Marx and Engels when they are describing changes in social structures. Organized social totalities 'give birth', 'bring into the world' a new type of organized totality that they bear within them, that 'comes to term' and is only brought forth in pain. This child-birth is simultaneously a filiation and a break, but there can only be filiation where there is a rending apart. Unity must be split in order to give birth to a new unity; there cannot be a better structure unless it grows out of a break in the old structure. The ideology of 'mutations' presupposes the mechanical alteration of a mechanism, in other words a spontaneous and automatic development affecting one by one the different parts of a composite. To avoid thinking of the general crisis as a necessary and determining moment in a given historical development, one must avoid thinking of the subject of the development, i.e. a given society, as an organic whole. Reformist mechanism articulates its conception of society; revolutionary dialectic does the same.

Crisis as Womb

One of the reasons why the successive stages or phases of a process like the transition to socialism or revolution cannot be schematized, cannot be in any way predetermined, is that the nature of each stage or phase is directly determined by the crisis which brings it about and the way in which that crisis is resolved. It is not enough to say that the transition from, say, capitalism to socialism involves one or more 'dangerous and decisive' crises which may affect the whole way the process goes, because 'the moment of crisis' is not something that can be isolated or neutralized, recognized as a definite milestone of any kind; it is part of the new process that is growing out of it, and throughout the development of that process it will remain the most strongly determining factor in its historical context. It is, if you like, the historical womb of that process, giving it its content and its character. (For instance 'on the basis of previous conditions' really means 'on the basis of the historical solutions of previous crises'.) The way in which a crisis has been resolved, or the way in which a social system has come into being, determines the form the next crisis will take and how it will be resolved, and shape the possibilities of approaching some new situation.

When crises occur, they seem to give history a kind of new life: it seems that anything might happen – we could begin everything all over again. But actually even in the most unexpected, least foreseeable crisis, there is a long memory at work, the memory of the womb. That is why the short period of the crisis is so decisive: it determines the crises of the future. That is why, too, there is an irreversible element in politics; it is not just that some revolutionary defeats can result in an irretrievable situation, but even victories, according to the conditions in which they have been won, can contain the seeds of defeats, or impasse situations, or regressions. And there can be defeats that are rich in promise for the future, good in the long term. Though the 'coup' or rather the 'counter-coup' in Prague in 1948 may have looked like a victory for socialism, the historical circumstances of that 'victory' showed the evolution (the process) which led to the Soviet intervention of August 1968 (the crisis). The events of 1968 were in the logic of 1948 – they were a kind of compensation, a deferred payment. A socialist régime that has not grown out of a profound and authentic revolutionary crisis, a crisis resolved on the basis of its own internal, national forces, through a long and difficult testing in history, is more than likely to carry within it the seeds of its own destruction – or at least of its distortion. To try to organize a revolution so as to create socialism in an ' economical','painless', 'satisfactory' manner, is merely to prepare the ground for a counter-revolution in the future.

In this sense, we can and must ask of every existing socialist regime: 'Tell me from what crisis you were born, and I will tell you what you are like. Tell me how, with the support of what determining social force, and on what battlefield you won power, and I will tell you what form of socialism you are constructing, and how.' It is because all the supposed theoreticians, experts or technicians of socialism tend to consider ' the transitional phase ' quite apart from its historical circumstances, that their economic science meanders from country to country so blindly and ineffectively, moving from incomprehension to failure. The historical circumstances are primarily the conditions in which the phase has its historical origin, in other words the revolutionary struggle in that particular country, through which the State power was won – conditions whose special form are determined by history, geography and culture. It is as non-dialectical, and as mistaken to erect ' the seizure of power ' into an absolute entity, identified with the revolution itself, as it is to discourse on ' the transitional phase' in general, as an economic interpretation of the problem which contains in itself everything that determines it autonomously and purely ' conceptually'. These supposed socialist experts also have a way of conceiving socialism as an autonomous and generic entity, defined by the system of its concepts, its ' scientific explanation of the problem'; and they move their gaze easily about the world from country to country, quite indifferent to each one's individual history, cultural identity and civilization; uninterested in the state of the productive forces, the collective outlooks, to say nothing of the political objectives which a given group of revolutionary leaders are pursuing; and these, after all, are not just 'the powers that be' but a group of leaders formed by and through their experience of this particular revolutionary struggle for power.

A ministerial crisis with street meetings (as in Prague), a long popular war of national liberation waged from country areas (as in China), a rising of workers in the capital (as in Petrograd), a diplomatic settlement between allies ultimately based on the determining weight of the Red Army (as in Eastern Europe), an autonomous national guerrilla war (as in Cuba and Vietnam); these are not merely totally different types of revolutionary direction, of work-style, of life-style, a pattern of identification for the masses which is different in each case. They are also what determine the kind of class alliances there will be, the identity of the social force effectively acting as the vanguard, the predominant role of the Army, or the Party, or a coalition of parties, in the running of the State. And the forms of the revolutionary struggle, which determine the nature and forms of subsequent socialist development, are themselves determined by the whole history of each society in the past, back to the way in which it emerged from the neolithic age into the historical era, and by its own particular socio-economic development.

The only socialist revolutions which allow of a development towards communism, a radicalizing of their political objectives and thereby the preservation of their socialist achievements (since these can only be preserved by continual advance), seem to be those which are ultimately based upon their own system of contradictions, those whose ' birth crisis ' was resolved from within – even though a complex totality of exterior causes may have contributed to their success (as with the imperialist war in 1917, for example).

I am of course speaking of this only in terms of what it makes *possible*: it is necessary, but it is not all that is necessary, as we see in the case of Tito's ultra-revisionist Yugoslavia. This situation of departure does not exist elsewhere in Eastern Europe; its development into a new type of capitalism is only a question of time, but that it *will* be a new type is beyond doubt, since there will certainly not be a mechanical return to any previous type. This inversion of which I am speaking is in a sense built into the origins of socialist power, because of the inevitable tension between national individuality and a socialism imported from outside which resulted from the historical circumstances prevailing after the war. Such contradiction, such historical discordance, tends to develop relentlessly in its effects, either in the resurgence of a nationalism that is anti-socialist, ' bourgeois' in character, though its supporters are working class, as in Czechoslovakia, or in a nationalistic socialism which sacrifices the remnants of proletarian internationalism on the altar of its own independence, as in Romania. What we are witnessing in each case is the delayed outburst of a contradiction that was dormant in the original 'crisis'; anything brought in from 'above' is artificial; the only thing that lasts is what comes from 'below'. The 'socialist camp' can be, and should be simply the common framework for all the various national socialisms, with all their own highly fertile individual differences; it cannot make demands which supersede national realities. It can, and must grow out of them.

*

It would be narrow, mistaken and indeed dangerous to expect to find the key to an entire historical period only in its 'crisis situations'. Such a restriction is out of the question. Just as antagonism is only a transitional element in the development of a contradiction, so a crisis is one atypical moment in an ongoing process, and can only be understood in relation to what follows on from it; though it may be the culminating point, what matters is the totality of the process. There can be no culminating point without the slope leading up to it; no summit is reached without an ascent. Very well then. But just as, in history as it actually happens, it is only in and through expressed antagonism that an antagonistic contradiction will be resolved one way or another, just as it is in and through a situation of general crisis that the decision emerges as to whether or not we are passing from the old to the new; so, at the level of reflection (of how we think about history as it happens), it is our consideration of the crisis moment which determines and clarifies a true theory of history. Only by clarifying a theory of history (general) through a theory of the crisis moment (particular) can that theory be preserved from the kind of mystified and mystificatory conception of the dialectic of history that I would call mysticism. That mysticism, we know, has acquired the name and form of 'mechanism' in the history of our movement. One may call mechanism a concept of contradictions as affecting the development of things in such a way that their resolution does not demand any form of 'crisis' – in the strongest and most ideological sense – of decision ($\kappa\rho\acute{\iota}o\iota\varsigma$). The contradictions themselves are responsible for their own solutions; they have not got to be 'decided' by conscious or political activity. They are resolved with a fatality, an inevitability, which nothing can alter.

Thus mechanism is a kind of short-cut, tending to remove the very need for politics, for the whole political process in structuring society, within the development of the economy. Mechanism is a concept of the revolutionary struggle which evades the need to think out that struggle as a strategy, in other words basically as something political, with the working out of possible decisions. The crisis moment is the strategic moment in the 'evolution of things', and it is also the moment which reveals the essence, the nature of politics – of one's opponent's politics, that is – as being strategic. It is in such moments of maximum intensity, such culminating points, that the basic reality of politics emerges: that basis is the direction of the class struggle, which is the art of confronting political crises, since that struggle is ultimately decided in the arena of the battle for State power.

In capitalist societies, mechanism expects revolutionary salvation from the periodic recurrence of economic crises. This is all bound up with an economic analysis, a discussion of the characteristic features of the present phase of the Western system, whereby one can determine the supposed regularity of and need for such crises, how to alleviate their worst effects, and so on. But what it is above all vital to see is that of itself an economic crisis is never strategic, and only becomes so when transposed to the political level; at the very most it can stage-manage the way the confrontation takes place, propose or modify the elements in the struggle, and achieve a favourable change in the balance of powers involved, though never entirely removing their margin for political manoeuvre. When Lenin said that there could never be an impasse for the bourgeoisie, he meant that there could always be some alternative, in other words that there is no economic determinism that can substitute for the people involved in the situation in deciding just how a given class conflict will be resolved. The crisis of 1923 in Germany was 'decided' by German financial capital in terms of fascism; it was not 'decided' in terms of socialism by the working class. The economic crisis 'proposed' a political battle to the vanguards of the two opposing sides – in highly unequal conditions, certainly – and it was politically lost for the working class by the leaders of their parties and their trade unions. No economic crisis makes it possible to get out of facing a political crisis; no amount of understanding of economic mechanisms dispenses anyone from studying how to conduct a political confrontation; one can never, in other words, be insured against the *possibility* of defeat.

Economism and mechanism are what one may call secular forms of a belief in pre-destination; in rose-coloured spectacles they imply a quasi-religious belief in inevitability. Gramsci has shown what a positive part they could play in periods of calm, as a popular philosophy, a kind of compensation ideology helping the revolutionary forces and the proletariat to overcome their discouragement, their sense of impotence, their failure to seize the moment. It permits the attitude: 'time is on our side; a longer run will give us a higher jump; the match is only postponed; etc.' It can equally be demonstrated how mechanism develops into triumphalism, after the conquest of power in the official ideology of the 'socialist camp'. The forces of progress march on, world-wide victory will soon be ours, capitalism is in its death throes, these are the final tortured heavings, and so on. The certainty that tomorrow all will be well makes it possible to let things take their course today; the poetry of the future makes it possible to tolerate the dreary administrative prose of the present, and thus, almost turning Gramsci upside down, the optimism of rational conviction obliges one to a pessimism of chosen behaviour. Mechanism then ceases to be an ideology leading on to action, a force for mobilizing energies, and becomes instead a de-mobilizing force justifying passivity. Hence that alternation of long periods of inertia with sudden wild bursts of life, of verbalist and dogmatic euphoria with panic responses to the crisis situations, whether internal or international, which characterize States where socialism is 'triumphant' (suffering and militant).

Some Irreverent Notes on the Hegelian Religion of History, and Some of its Effects (Freely Interpreted)

Mechanism in all its varying forms may be considered to be the most direct effect of purely and simply overthrowing Hegelian dialectic. It is the spiritualist dialectic set right way up, on its feet, walking not on its ideas, but on the development of its productive forces. It is through Hegel as intermediary, the Hegelian philosophy of history taken literally (and turned upside down, though the spirit is unchanged), that one kind of Marxism becomes once again affiliated to the religions of the Book. I must say at once that what I mean is an organic descent, from within, on the side of pseudo-Marxism 'as a science', and not some external element of religion resulting from transforming a system of ideas into a popular belief, a mass ideology, a force for social cohesion – as indeed every religion is through its succession of great mediators (Mao, the red sun, the eternal, the thousand years, etc.). This aspect of things relates to historical study, to sociology; the affiliation I am talking of relates to philosophy.

1. To Hegel, the general concept of the philosophy of history is that it is the manifestation of reason, which is simply that manifestation whereby it becomes reunited with itself in a unity of spirit. Just as Wisdom achieves its ends in the world, Hegelian Reason is a coherent providence, a providence logical in its own terms to the last degree. Hegel criticizes the Christian idea of Providence (as in Bossuet), not for what it is, but because it fails to be known. He wants only to reveal what is hidden, to penetrate the impenetrable ways of God by Reason. Reason then becomes a profane Providence, because it is open to every philosophical gaze,

but profoundly sacred too, because it transcends all the individual moments that go to make up its happening. The absolute is movement, that movement is history, and that history is something that can be known. Therefore Hegel is going to know God (the absolute Idea). In his *Dialectical Notebooks*, Lenin often contrasts Hegel and his wish to increase the power of science, with Kant, who tries to exalt religious faith at the expense of science. But Hegelian dialectic starts by getting rid of the divisions between science and faith, and the object of science and the object of faith; it is through this dialectic that God is giving himself to be known. Thus evidently there can be no more contingency in what is known, and any contradiction can only be provisional.

The Spirit makes use of History as a vehicle for self-expression, to move from being in-itself (*en-soi*) to being for-itself (*pour-soi*), in other words to become what it is through a series of contradictions; but all there is in itself is the desire to be reconciled with itself, and thus bring to an end the contradiction. The contradictions of history as it actually happens are contradictions by default, so to say, the forms of transition of a unity whose arrival will mark the end of History – in other words the end of all contradiction. For Marxism such an end can have no meaning, unless there is some kind of pre-existing simple essence acting as the force behind the historical process. There will never be an end to the development of human society; it will never stop working to achieve its unity, or rather, it will achieve it only by way of a succession of indefinitely renewed contradictions. Which is precisely the reason why 'human society' can never exist in reality except in the plural, in societies, in individual nations, in various civilizations, etc. (It will be interesting to see how the twenty-first century treats the national problem: whether there will be greater world-wide unity, stronger identity of national bodies, a closer similarity in living conditions – technological, scientific, economic or a greater accentuation of differences – cultural linguistic, psychological. Indeed there is no end to this dialectic between the specific and the universal.)

2. This providential inevitability, guiding the way the Spirit

develops in time, theoretically presupposes a model of *creative* causality. The Idea is the *creator* of Nature, which is more or less what the Great Logic tells us (I cannot give precise quotations). The essence produces physical reality as its phenomenon, just as reason engenders the history of phenomena, the story of what actually happened to the people who have figured in it in turn, from east to west. The philosophy of history then consists in drawing phenomena back to their inner essence, their One Cause, just as Bossuet imputed the death of the young Henrietta of England to the Will of God.

3. Even though, for Hegel, in the order of knowledge 'no one can advance beyond his time', in fact simple determination by an 'internal principle' means the same as pre-determination. The reality of history, with its natural, geographical, accidental and other determinations, merely demonstrates this; there is nothing further it can add. It cannot therefore teach the philosopher of history anything the philosopher does not already know – all it can teach him is his own philosophy. The simplicity of creative causality makes it possible to separate the essential conditions for a phenomenon's existence, or in materialist–historical terms, the determination by the infra-structure of the complex collection of super-structural, social, ideological, juridical, political and other determinations. That is how dogmatism works to arrive at the idea of a general law as a need to be fulfilled independent of the particular circumstances through which it is fulfilled, circumstances which remain external and neutral to it and in no way compelling. That is why dogmatism can say nothing of 'existing reality' as such; all it can do is validate it, recognize its conformity with the 'dialectical' necessity of which it is merely an exposition, even if to do so means cutting away some part of the reality which does not fit in with its 'essence'.[1] In genetic terms, there is a

1. cf. Garaudy's articles on Cuba in 1962, in which he shows that the Cuban revolution is a 'splendid application of the well-known laws of dialectic, though it inevitably has its own special qualities of the kind which limit all great principles when they actually become embodied in concrete reality, like the negation of negation', etc.

pre-formationist inside every dogmatist. In the eighteenth century a man's entire future was believed to exist in germ in the homunculus in the womb. The only difference was a change in dimensions, his features merely becoming visible through enlargement. Similarly the future of a social structure is there to see in its embryo-contradiction, the opposition between production relationships and productive forces, which is a miniature reflection of its whole future development. The pre-formationist does not accept living reality as a dialectical unity between the organism and the conditions in which it exists, between its genetic make-up and its environment; the theologian of history does not recognize an existing historical reality as a dialectical unity between its own principle of development and the circumstances enabling it to exist.

*

What appears as predetermined, predestined, for Hegel and his disciples is this:

In the development of history, a succession of moments through which the Spirit unfolds, there is a fusion of events and values, of the order of time and the order of importance. What is logically consecutive – i.e. the order of the succession of events – is objectively superior. (For Hegel objectively means spiritually; with spiritual reality back on its feet, you have what is 'socially' superior.) The Spirit, like a snowball, rolls in the element of nature, amassing more and more spirit and thus creating history. It rolls along through the periods of successive civilizations, enlarging itself through its own activity, by a kind of substantial spontaneity, and what is added is an interiorization. All the while it is growing, it continues to get closer to itself, to that moment when by at last coming into contact with its own essence, it will relax the spring of history, and reach the moment of rest and calm possession. This will be absolute knowledge, the end of history. This is the 'snowball' effect of history (designated by Althusser as 'cumulative interiorization'); the process of the Spirit's progressive self-determination, from the most abstract to the most concrete. There is therefore necessarily, obligatorily, something to add to the total instant t' as compared with the previous state of the totality t, and that extra something is a 'closerness to itself', something better. (And it is this necessity that provides the basic necessity in the Hegelian dialectic: one need know nothing of the circumstances to make one's affirmation.)

In such conditions, the royal road of world history is a one-way street, and that one way is most profound reality. The Spirit can neither stand still nor go backwards. To Hegel and those who have come after him, it is meaningless to talk in terms of a standstill in history, still more a regression: it is meaningless, and therefore can have no reality. It is inconceivable that movement should go from plus to minus, from the more to the less concrete. Medieval Christianity was the setting up, the setting in operation of the principle of individual subjectivity, of the personal soul; the principle of the individual was its essential element. Since that element both included and transcended in itself the Roman principle of the abstract juridical individual, it could not go back on what it had gained once and for all; that would not be just to deny its own condition for existing, but also to attack its own essence, the movement whereby that essence was preserved through its successive negations. Indeed what is quite unthinkable from a Hegelian point of view is any discord between the conditions in which historical action occurs and the goal for which it may be working: equally impossible is to conceive of any Utopia resulting from such discord. The old contains in itself the seeds of the new, the present contains the future as its own development; so much so that for men to become aware of the new means that it has now actually arrived. In this sense, the Marxist idea that mankind only asks itself questions that it can answer, or for which it has already got the key to the answer, would seem to be a direct descendant of Hegelian rationalism.

But does that rationalism allow for failure as a basic possibility inherent in all historical activity? Surely one must admit the thought of failure with all it involves ('In what conditions could historical failure be a possibility?') if one is to understand success, to know just what it costs, to relate it correctly to the conditions that make it possible. Surely a certain mystical concept of social development, that euphoria which has enabled a large part of the workers' movement (and that the part that is precisely the least combative, readiest for compromise, for waiting-and-seeing, for class collaboration) to live through a century of optimistic, verbose, high-sounding and meaningless speeches – surely that concept must in fact bear the responsibility for a great many setbacks, disappointments, periods of stagnation and indeed regression? Marx and Engels themselves, in their historical studies, whenever they had to consider a definite period in the class struggle in Europe, firmly turned their back first on Hegel, and then on the whole mystique of the 'historical sense' that owes its origins to him. When it came to historical reality, they dealt only with premature attempts at revolution, those precisely in which all the necessary conditions did not come together – they never do – in which allowance had to be made for imponderables, for chance, and so on. So it was with the Commune, and with 1848. After all, Engels actually showed, in *The Peasant Wars*, how a political vanguard can, in the haze of a false religious awareness, end up by recognizing a goal that is genuinely revolutionary, but beyond its reach.

The tragedy of Münzer is not just one of history's oddities, nor is it simply a piece of national folklore. Often a proletarian vanguard or a group of revolutionary leaders have found themselves caught in the kind of objective impasse in which they have been obliged to undertake a certain action in the full awareness that conditions were such as to make success impossible; they have done it precisely because, as Marx said of the Commune, not to undertake it, to run away, would at that time and in those circumstances, be an even worse disaster. As for the difference between what *should* be done and what *can* be done, we have of course to try our best to reduce it, not to see it as immutable fate, and avoid forcing a direct confrontation even though one knows it may well prove to be insoluble. Lenin had no liking for the theoretical concepts – the spontaneism, the obliviousness to the problem of nationalism, the democratism, etc. – of Rosa Luxemburg. But he uttered no word of blame for her having launched herself so wholeheartedly into the Spartacus rising – a rising of which she herself was chary, and indeed expected to fail. Then, in the conditions in Germany in 1919, her duty as a revolutionary was to take the lead in that probable failure. In other words, one's duty can only be defined as the need of that particular moment of history theoretically understood and physically entered into, carried to its ultimate conclusion.

A spiritualistic, naturalistic dialectic which, on the other hand, proposes to control the time of historical reality ends up by making it totally unintelligible. If the socialist system is consecutive, and thus superior to the capitalist system, it is not 'conceivable' that socialism should, for instance, ever evolve into a new type of capitalism; that would be a development 'against nature', and would therefore have to be the result of an intervention from an external, artificial cause, fomented by an outside enemy. Then this 'historical materialism' has got back to an idealist–conspiratorial concept of history. Within the socialist camp, in the glorious phase of construction, etc., the negative is inessential; it cannot even develop out of the positive. It is either a survival from the past with the return in force of the former exploiting class, or a conspiracy, or in most cases, both. Therefore the solution to this form of contradiction falls to the police (or the Army), giving the people back to themselves, restoring their awareness of their true interests which have for a time been obscured by false leaders abusing the good faith of others, etc.

The theory that the movement to socialism is an irreversible historical act which morally commits an entire given society to itself – or, failing that, to other socialist countries – involves us in a complete metaphysic of development. Quite apart from the strategic interests of the major power under threat, there is a reasoning which goes from theory to fact, from the logic of history to its embodiment in the immediate reality of society.

II Schema for a Study of Gramsci[1]

1

His historicism can be turned against him, in the sense that he too can be subjected to a historically limitative analysis. Indeed, he cannot be understood outside his specific historical context, or divorced from the object of his opposition.

i) Gramsci's fundamental target was 'social–democratic' and 'Bukharinist' mechanism which he saw as a form of fatalism, as a confusion between the science of nature and the science of history (hence his anti-Engelsian, anti-scientific emphasis).

What was the principal danger? The principal confusion *against* which and in relation to which Gramsci's position was to be defined and Marxism was to be distinguished? Defining the particularity, i.e. the inner essence of a doctrine or theory is something which cannot be done abstractly: it is an active and reactive operation. To define means to distinguish, to separate from a historical environment, from a filiation, from a threatening affinity. Gramsci sets out to establish the nature of Marxism as compared to the mechanistic materialism of the eighteenth century. He is therefore engaged in a struggle: the character of his theoretical work is essentially polemical, just as his activity as a militant is founded on that theoretical work. It is wrong to try and 'excuse' certain of Gramsci's theoretical formulations, however surprising they may be, as deriving from his situation as an active militant. This is what Cogniot does in the *Morceaux Choisis*[2]; he is continually seeking to defend Gramsci from himself, to 'moderate' him as if trying to calm down a person who has become over-excited in the heat of a dispute. In reality, all theoretical analysis is of its very essence polemical, a 'committed' form

1. This English translation is taken from the *New Left Review*.
2. The title is in fact: Antonio Gramsci, *Œuvres Choisies*, published by Éditions Sociales, with an introduction by Georges Cogniot.

of critique; Marx himself constructs *Capital* on a critique of political economy, starting from – and against – Smith, Ricardo and Say. The interesting thing in Gramsci's case is that he does not hide it, he does not claim any scholarly, academic or 'scientific' 'objectivity', he lays his cards on the table: he theoretically assumes the necessity for explicit polemic.

ii) In this struggle, Gramsci takes as his starting-point (i.e. turns for assistance to) Croce, Sorel, De Man: authors – especially Croce – whose importance he over-estimates. This over-estimation too (in our eyes) is a historical feature, the mark of an epoch.

2

These limitations notwithstanding, the immense merit of Gramsci is that he took as the central node and strategic junction of his analyses the unity, the welding together of theory and praxis. That he radically opposed any separation of the two. Gramsci is the man who asks himself how theory can make the *transition* into history; anybody who is a genuine militant, seeking to act in a revolutionary manner, necessarily comes up against this problem of how to effect a fusion of history and philosophy. A fusion:

i) *From the revolutionary–political point of view:* unity between 'spontaneity' and 'conscious leadership' (Turin council movement), relation between party and masses, leaders and rank-and-file militants. (The passage on p.338 is an extraordinarily apt prescription for the May movement: i.e. do not condemn it but raise it above itself.[1]) The party = *education* = collective intellectual (the party 'as' collective intellectual); or the contradiction negated: the intellectual in fact *is* the individual.

ii) *From the theoretical point of view:* 'modern theory can be in opposition to the spontaneous feelings of the mass', 'as a quantitative difference, not one of quality'. Marxism effects a junction with common sense: it surpasses and resumes it.

1. op. cit., p. 338, corresponding to A. Gramsci, *Passato e Presente*, Einaudi, p. 57.

iii) *From the cultural point of view:* 'the intellectuals' must be evaluated according to whether they do or do not constitute a link with the ascendant masses. If they do, they are 'organic', if not, they are artificial.

iv) *From the artistic point of view:* popular literature. How is the bond achieved between literature and people? What is the form in which a people or nation can accede to the literature of the élite? Hence Gramsci's meticulous attention to the historical reality of the nation, inseparable from the theoretical moment. Marxism must be born of a historical implantation, must continue a tradition – and this in its *incarnated* form. Thus it must 'translate' the concreteness of life into theoretical form. ('A scholastic, academic, conception of history and of politics is the expression of a passivity.'[1] Historically correct.) *Translate* common sense into philosophy and *incorporate* (Marxist) philosophy into common sense: these are the two key precepts. The question of the *transition* from one to the other, understood at once as translation and transformation.

3

We have an extraordinary historical advantage over Gramsci. For Gramsci was not destined to see the 'transition' of Marxism into a concrete historical society. He could not assess the consequences – both for Marxism and for Russian society. We, however, have watched fifty years of a fantastic historical experiment: what happens to a theory when it has become the official ideology of a number of states? Or again, what happens to a culture when a 'scientific' theory has been incorporated into it? Etc.

At this point, a note: the Marxists. Marxism has not yet reflected upon its own incarnation in history. During the past fifty years, socialism has become a historical, social and cultural reality for one-third of the world's population: the 'countries with a socialist system', what used to be called the 'socialist

1. See Cogniot, p. 339, *Passato e Presente*, p. 58.

camp'. This half century constitutes a history, which has produced a resultant. This history is a complex one, and consequently its resultant is complex too. It is not the superficial expression of a simple principle; there are different levels, inequalities, contradictions between the levels, both within a single country and between the various countries – economic, cultural and political contradictions. But the fact that the reality is a complex one means that a complex analysis is necessary, and not that all analysis can be dispensed with!

Now, this socialist 'realization' (history as resultant) has not been the object of a Marxist analysis. For various reasons:

i) Marxism is not the analysis of socialism, but of the capitalist system. The hiatus is especially evident in the field of economics: despair of the socialist economists searching laboriously for references in Marx (Gotha Programme, Manifesto, Correspondence, etc.).

ii) The historical necessities of struggle have given priority to defence over knowledge: first of all, defend the socialist camp from its assailants in order to protect the proletariat from doubt and despair, etc. Hence apology rather than analysis. Impossibility of taking a distance. For it is evident that analysis would reveal the existence of contradictions internal to socialism; contradictions which communism – as a mass ideology – claims have disappeared.

iii) It would necessarily involve using 'heterodox' concepts: civilization, culture, etc.

iv) The way in which consciousness, and science too, lag behind the process that is their object.

4

Gramsci is simultaneously philosopher 'and' historian: (even from the point of view of simple quantity, he left as many philosophical notes as historical ones). But he is neither a historian of philosophy – which would presuppose that philosophy can have a history of its own, comprehensible from within itself (an anti-Gramscian, idealist premise). Nor is he a philosopher of history – which would presuppose a dissolution of real history into some philosophical teleology (another anti-Gramscian premise). The problem which he confronts is contained in that 'and'; Gramsci stands on the watershed between *relation* and *distinction*. Instead of seeing relation as given once and for all, he presents it as a problem, or rather as problems in the plural – in the sense of problems that each time are new, unique, 'historical'. History as a problem to solve: that is Gramsci's strength. His weakness, or better his historicist deviation, appears whenever he treats history as its own solution, as a self-solving problem: 'Humanity never poses itself problems other than those which it can solve, problems the conditions for whose solution do not already exist ...'; this is the motif which continually recurs. Whence certain doubts: how and why historicism is not a simple historical relativism. Also certain lacunae: how and why science can exist, etc. There is a further objective limit of history, which gives certain of Gramsci's texts their pathos (though it by no means robs their value – they remain to bear witness, milestones of a historical hope): the texts which predict, which expect from the 'transition' of theory into practice a new civilization, a new culture, a way of life, a scale of values radically different from those prevalent under Western capitalism – which has become inorganic, decadent, dualist. As far as Europe (USSR and People's Democracies) is concerned, history has frustrated these hopes. The Gramscian task for us today is to seek out the reasons, the modalities and the consequences of that frustration. 'Gramscian' because it particularly concerns Europe, the Italian and French workers and intellectuals. Some of the political conditions exist, especially in Italy, for beginning this work. But the objective dynamic of the theoretical field (thrusts and counter-thrusts) will necessarily tend to displace this criticism towards the right – 'revisionism' – to the extent that it seeks its points of reference in Europe alone. Or else at the opposite extreme, the criticism will seek its points of reference solely in the myths of the Third World or in a non-European reality, and it will then be displaced in the direction of a romantic, abstract leftism, without roots or points of application in the sphere of reality. Is it possible to overcome this alternative, this mutual incomprehension of two positions which are equally incorrect (the right-wing position is a mass one, the left-wing position is one of minorities trapped in a ghetto) but sufficiently displaced to justify each other reciprocally, to feed each other's reason for existing? Judging by events – by what is happening in Rome or Paris – one would not say so.

(By 'reality' I mean phenomena seen critically, restored to their effective conditions of possibility. The drama of 'May 1968' is that it is already fulfilling the same function for left extremism as 'June 1936' fulfilled for communist reformism: the function of a justificatory myth, the residue of decades of illusions. What is new in comparison with 1936 is the speed with which the phenomenon made the transition from history to myth, from the real to the symbolic. This is of course due to the progress made by capitalism in its ability to recuperate those who were contesting its power, by means of books, newspapers, films, plays, etc. But above all May succeeded in satisfying a real need, an immense frustrated need, felt by revolutionary groups (and also to a certain degree by the entire social body) as something to be exorcized, rejected. This was precisely the need for Myth, for an autochthonous Myth, internal to capitalism – without forgetting that every myth reflects a relative rupture as an absolute. This need was born of the hiatus produced by the imbalance between an immediate, local, grey, reformist profane history and the breath of revolution, a disruptive yet mediated and distant force (China, Vietnam, Cuba) – without the two moments being able to meet on the ground of the *hic et nunc*. The hiatus was filled by what took on the appearance of a reality: the myths born of May 1969. The need is satisfied for twenty years.

Some Literary Reflections

In Settlement of All Accounts[1]

Garrison of La Esperanza,
May–June 1967

At last the sentry has opened one side of the shutter. But I can hardly look at the sky; it is so bright this morning that it dazzles your eyes like gleaming metal. I see a flat, bare field, a dirt path leading to the sentry-post, a low white hut with a door in the middle. How marvellous it is to be able to look at things and run one's eyes over them and list them like this! In a line from my cell there are three palm-trees and two umbrella-pines standing out black against the light. They are rustling in the breeze – it sounds rather like the noise an hour-glass makes as the sand runs through. To the right is a little roof of Roman tiles, the wash house to which they take me at night. Far behind, standing out against a high wall of sugar cane in flower there is a deserted road. I really can't imagine what state secret they have been trying to hide from me by keeping me in the dark. All I can see is a scene of relaxation and peace, a holiday scene, the kind of summer country landscape I might see at home. Framed by the window, it is a very ordinary picture of happiness, as fragile and precious as one of those forgotten memories you can sometimes recapture for a moment by shutting your eyes, and try to hold on to for as long as you can. It would be so easy to slip out between the bars and drive along that country road in a little Citroën to go and do the shopping in the next village . . .

The wind, already getting warmer, is beginning to come through the windows, and you can feel it on your skin. It is early morning. You can smell just the same scent of dried lavender you get in the summer in the stony country of Haute Provence, up on the plateaux. A speckled thrush flies up out of a thicket. I hear a harsh and familiar cackle beside me. Why should this handful of smells and colours suddenly come at me, full blast? Why should life feel

1. Translated from an unpublished typescript.

so real and so close so near its end? Warm, heavy memories seem to hold one to the earth like leaden soles, to be riveted by the light. I realize I must not let this heaviness take possession of me, that these vivid sensations from the past barely deserve a moment's regret. There must, surely, be some more important, more attractive reality than the pull of merely physical happiness, some reality that will enable us to leave that behind with a light heart. If only they will allow me the time to express what I feel, to get it down on to paper!

May is already over – the sentry told me the date through the window, though he has strict orders not to speak to the prisoner. I had completely lost count for, in warding off a blow from a stick at the very beginning, I broke my watch, which also told me the date. It was a stupid reflex – knowing the time is far more important than parrying just one blow, when there would be more to come. How many days had I spent in the dark? Or rather how many weeks? With news of no one, left only to daydream, lying on my back, chained to my camp-bed with sharp bits of the mattress springs sticking into my bottom, I had only the ignoble occupation of feeling my own body, reminding myself of who I was, and what I was doing there, and what precisely had happened. At the mercy of my own confused memories, drifting about in a senseless, shapeless time, in which minutes would seem hours, and then hours minutes. Total isolation makes one lose all sense of time. Either it passes far too quickly in those periods of fevered delight when you are expecting the execution squad not merely with impatience but with a kind of aggressive exaltation; or it passes terribly slowly as in those periods of exquisite bitterness when you try to gather up every detail of your memories with a morose fascination, going back again and again over the same ground, reviewing the sequences of the past, rearranging past plans, rectifying past mistakes, endlessly reviewing your least movements like some lunatic film-director who keeps running through the reel of his life over and over again until he makes it come out exactly as he wants, doing everything he should do, and the life can then move on in its precise and predictable groove. No passport problems, all contacts punctual to the minute, all the wheels oiled, nothing unexpected, rather like those all too perfect stories we hear from members of the Resistance – those who survived, that is – who foolishly recount their deeds of prowess without any notion of what a large part luck had to play in the whole thing.

The order to untie me and let the light into my cell came this morning. Now they will only chain me down again at night, for sleeping. I have light, paper, ballpoint pen – all I need for a well-ordered life. I can ask for nothing more. Not a minute to lose. It would have been hard to have to go without having settled my accounts. My own past demands it. I have had no books for some time, and it hardly bothered me. But to go without leaving any-thing behind would be bad. An intellectual is first and foremost someone who draws up his accounts as regularly as a shopkeeper, only in his case they are the accounts of his states of mind. These particular ones are not quite up to date. Now it is impossible to put anything off till the future. Here I am with my back to the wall, forced to rush my way through a short history which should have been written in philosophical leisure. Shaking off my indolence, I must assemble all my ghosts, get dead ideas into order with everyday words, which are all I have, however vague and inapt they may be. Twenty-six is rather a funny age to set about writing Memoirs, even though one may not feel any certainty of living to be twenty-seven. Memories don't interest me. Though I recall a few now, it is only to help me discover what has happened to the high hopes of my adolescence, what separates me from them now, what still links me with them, and what name to give to this new and not very impressive position I have now reached. They are all so many signposts through the labyrinth. My two daily bowls of soup and my well-escorted visit to the lavatory hardly constitute remarkable adventures to relate, so I must draw a line with my ballpoint and try to add it all up.

My earliest memories are not of a garden, a hillside or a human face, but of the printed word; those tall, thick volumes of Hertzel, with their faded red bindings and once-gold titles, that were so dusty as to make you sneeze; the Jules Vernes with their white pages, printed in tiny compact print, and scattered with brownish spots like the hands of old men, or like the marks left by stubbed-out cigarette-ends; the *Histoire de la Révolution* by Louis Blanc, with the streaky illustrations which added a dramatic note to the September Massacres, or the last *Agapes* of the Girondins in the Concièrgerie, combining the pathos of photographs with the tranquillity of colour-prints; the ancient six-volume Larousse, falling to pieces, with titles and headings in something resembling German gothic script, and its green board binding all unstuck.

Though I must have managed to decipher these and other similar works at a very early age, I should be unable to say anything about their content now. I remember what they looked like, what they weighed, how they smelt; I remember the crick in my neck from lying on my tummy on the carpet reading them – but of what was in them I remember nothing. Our individual pre-history, like that of civilization, is closed in on itself, embedded silently in the rocks of time; it is like a clam that won't open. Yet that, which leaves no trace, and is lost from the memory, it is that that will guide the hands of the adult, and make him write in one way rather than another. Books! The first artificial satellites launched by men, not so much to improve communications between them as to enter into the general competition – each trying to plant his own little flag higher in the space of time, cherishing the illusion that he will never wholly disappear from the world as long as his books go on being read after he dies. And here am I writing too, as though I really had no alternative; as though I too wished to plant my own little flag, as a cross or a sheaf of flowers, in memory. But I shall plant it in the earth, this strange earth reflecting the blue of the sky, with palm-trees like giant feather-dusters stuck in the ground, sugar-canes a field of waving white in the wind, and the mountains on the horizon where comrades are dying for what they believe in. I shall plant my flag near here, well knowing that it will disappear when I do in the night.

I am writing because they have told me I may die soon – they keep telling me so. I wonder whether that is really such bad news. I am not writing to redeem my life. If it has been valueless, then no words I can string together now will make any difference to that. I no longer look to words to provide me with music; I want them to be as dry as figures in an annual balance-sheet. I no longer want to serve them, but I want them to serve me. Now. And it matters little whether they are forgotten tomorrow along with their writer. What a lot of time to waste serving an apprentice-ship to the obvious! What use was Paris, and all those years so poorly spent living as a student among students, an imitation teacher among real professors, a failed philosopher alongside genuine intellectuals – all my erstwhile friends?

Paris, ten years ago:
Born into the bourgeoisie, and not needing to earn our living by dirtying our hands, we thought we could analyse our world and our hearts at arm's length, so to speak. With the help of time and all the long words we had learnt, they would readily yield up their secrets, and these we could accept at face value. By teaching us to discriminate among things, to know every detail about colours, doctrines, plants, professions, and even our own feelings, our wide vocabulary made our senses keener and intensified everything in our lives. With the academic year measuring out our seasons and weeks, we could stroll round the streets of the Latin Quarter with nothing to worry about except ourselves and our salvation, each his own, each for himself. We realized that we were dedicated to a solitary venture, for we saw our own lives first and foremost as an admirable contrast – a good book, a better book than the others. We found the mediocrity all about us splendid, since our brilliance would show up all the more clearly against it and draw fuel from it. And as we roamed about the Sorbonne in groups, as we met to found a magazine, or work out a manifesto, or drink a beer, I am convinced that every one of us wanted to be the first to draw away from the rest to shine more brightly alone.

Who were we? Close friends and then less close, then colleagues – students and teachers – a whole group of young people each one longing to establish a unique and necessary niche, possibly objectively recognizable as such, but certainly so recognized by their fellows. How far away, how comically far they now seem to me, even though it was all so few years ago! Yet we grew up together, or at least we pretended to grow up, hiding our childishness under a veneer of grown-up talk. Our regular inspection of all the bookshop windows told us what was going on in the world far more reliably than any newspaper, and gave us far fewer surprises. It was always going on well. Ink was flowing freely everywhere, and every month it cast up at our feet printed matter by the ton, all as announced and described in the previous month's catalogues. All we had to do was make sure we got the title right, skim through the first pages, leaf through the volumes, and take the best of them home – usually paying for them, for we were not hard up. To be a consumer of culture is skilled work and not easy, but it was our job, and we were used to it. The certainty each of us felt that he was working for himself and thus securing his future as a producer gave our appetite for the printed word a certain keenness, almost possessiveness. Everyone wanted to be the one who collected the most books soonest, to be the first to find a helpful second-hand bookseller when a particular collection of Ganguilhem's articles turned out to be unobtainable, the first to get to Vrin[1] in time to grab the last Aristotle from an edition now out of print, or one particular volume of the younger Marx's works, published by the now long-defunct Costes. Once such treasures had been acquired, established firmly in the recesses of our memory and on the shelves of our *thurnes*,[2] there to remain, we could let time take its course with no fears for the morrow. We were quite sure that all these books would pay dividends, providing us with an income for life. Our capital was working for us, and time was on our side. Of course there would come a time when it was our turn to publish something, and show the stuff of which we were made. Later we could bring out our wealth from the safe-deposits we kept it in, and the greater the astonishment of an ill-informed public, the greater our success would be. Some deceitful people would try to

1. Vrin is the French university bookshop.
2. The bedroom-studies in the École Normale Supérieure in the Rue d'Ulm were known by this name.

keep their wealth a secret and pretend to an ignorance their circle knew to be feigned, putting off publishing anything, and gloating over their silence like misers rubbing their hands at the thought of the interest mounting on their money. Whether it was genuine laziness or fear of inadequacy hardly mattered. For we all dreamed dreams of power and what we were really thinking about as we enthused noisily over the work of others was our own future works – though to have admitted this would have been breaking the rules of the game.

We would often talk about such writers as Dos Passos and Svevo for hours on end round a café table, sitting there for the whole afternoon. Then, sometimes, when it was evening, first one and then another would become subject to a highbrow weariness, and wander off dreaming down the streets, tired and bored, as though they had already written their own novels, and as though all that talk and argument had been a waste of time since their work was done. And they were right, in a sense: the cards *were* already on the table. A great many knew just where their books would be displayed behind that plate-glass. Some of our friends already had places there, and the rest soon would have. It was our birthright that our wealth should grow of itself; we had but to await our turn. All we could envisage, though, was the happy ending. Used as we were to the comforts of city living, we had become accustomed, like everyone else, to the finished product appearing as we wanted, delivered to our doorstep; we had lost all contact with the long and messy process of producing them. We gathered the lovely polished fruits, accepting them as our due, without even a thought, without their costing us any more than the money that cost us nothing. There were girls with willing bodies, soft and silky, never tired, always fashionably dressed, every one of them ready to be kissed and forgotten in turn; food fell from the heaven first of the family, then of the State, arriving regularly on our plates three times a day, hot and punctual; clean sheets every Saturday, an eiderdown to keep us warm, sheltered from the rain and cold outside. Then there were the art galleries in nearby towns in Italy and Holland, where we could go by car in summer or train in winter, without any effort on our part: and above all, the books, with their shiny covers, smelling deliciously of glue and fresh ink, there on the shelves where our greedy fingers could reach them.

What did all this ease of living make of us? Physical weaklings, suffering for lack of earth, sky, and manual labour. Minor officials of capitalism and its legalized robbery, born of the cowards' peace and everyone else's war. Profiteers who could talk of nothing but rebellion. With all the neon signs and luxury revues, and unthinking mockery, and deep concern over our holidays, we never saw the world's shadowy underside, the way the other half lives, the half who pay for our artificial lights. And we went round and round the streets of Paris, that cage of wolves, by turns stuffed and starving, without realizing that we were moving within four walls, and that all our ambitions were like the daydreams of prisoners. I feel freer in the cell I am in now than I was then. In those days we had all the bloodsuckers of the adolescent on our heels – we were the helpless prey of eroticism, little in-groups, literary journalism and the film libraries. Whatever the present-day substitutes for these things may be, I don't suppose they are any better.

The cinema, that other bloodsucker, would land beauty in our laps whenever we wished, for a few pieces of silver. We could afford to enjoy it several times a week. And that is not counting those crisis days when our satisfied and yet insatiable desire made us spend whole afternoons and evenings in its darkness. No sooner had we come out, scarcely had we left its embrace, our eyes still half-blind, than we would sit round a café table going over every detail of the phantom body, as mercilessly and crudely as regular customers of a brothel – then back to the screen again, sunk deep into our front-row seats. The cinema, which is the ultimate crystallization of the division of people into spectators and magicians, works so as to give every newcomer the sense of having crossed over the line and somehow become a kind of creator himself, or at least of being capable of becoming one some day if he so wishes. I think that is where its real magic lies. Simple souls identify with great muscular stars, making love to Lana Turner or

Brigitte Bardot. But we were sophisticated enough to think more of the directors, and look far more at the camera than the film. And how could anyone fail to envy them, those gods behind their dark glasses and their public image, as they do their work on the montage and create the world as they wish? From our reading of specialist magazines, having a friend or two in the profession, our occasional visit to the studios, we knew some of their gimmicks, and tried to feel some share in the work of creation, not just as spectators but as critics. With great self-assurance we told them where they had gone wrong. The film library was close at hand, and in a few years it had turned us, like so many thousands of others, into the grammarians of modern beauty, its chroniclers and its purists. The idea that *October* or *The Birth of a Nation* had actually been made to arouse anger and hatred did not really strike us. Only historical accident could justify such lack of artistry. These so-called 'messages', flung so apparently ingenuously at the audience, disturbed us above all (they could only be called messages in the sense of providing some amount of information to be decoded, but that was not the context in which they appeared here). How could we ever have guessed that there was a time when challenging strangers, stirring up a crowd, summoning help or calling people to take up arms was once as vital as swimming or breathing – or rather that it was another expression of the same need, the need to live? To us it was no more than a discomfort, the sound of a car backfiring during a concert. Determinedly we discussed the montage, tracking shots, lighting, rhythms.

There were directors, unknown to the wider public, whose names I have now forgotten, who let slip these passwords to the in-group of film enthusiasts. Are they still remembered, these names we went such distances to see? Masterpieces and geniuses in this sphere are few and far between. For a single incredible flash, the dominant yellow tone in a colour sequence, the uncut version of an artistically prolonged *plan fixe*, we would venture as far afield as le Temple, Clichy or la Bastille; we would even sit through a film that was dubbed. For it was the American cinema that delighted us most. Westerns, thrillers, musical comedies, would give us two hours with a lovely long-legged girl in black net tights, or gun-slinging enemies, so that at times, with the help of the darkened cinema, we seemed to reach those ultimates we could get at in no other way – love and death. We might feel a little ashamed of our excitement afterwards. We would hasten to explain it in terms of visual fascination, and would certainly never admit to anyone else what we had really felt. Our commentaries on what we had seen were always strictly at a technical level. 'Plastic' was the great word. Our task was made easier by such standardized classifications, with their rigid and codified conventions.

It may well be the case that our best and most sincere moments were those spent in front of the screen. It would often happen, though I don't quite know how, that those fake windows would really open, and we managed to breathe genuine fresh air through them. So small was our cage, so stifled were we, that the slightest black and white diversion would bring us back to ourselves. To be honest: we could not lie to ourselves in the dark; with no one watching, we could give way to our bodies and those curiously strong emotions which, even though you might swallow the lump in your throat, still brought tears to your eyes. There were some films which cut right through our defences and left us shaking – like those half-waking dreams when one cannot decide whether it is more painful to abandon oneself totally to the dream-state or put an end to it by forcing oneself awake. The best of all frightened us as fortune-tellers might. They were our own confessions acted out in pictures, and seeing them was more than we could bear. In the cinema, more than anywhere, beauty is always painful. *Senso, Le Fleuve, La Guerre est finie,* Wajda's *Love at Twenty, A Place in the Sun, Jules et Jim, Il terrorista* (in which the key man in the network murmurs ' Nessuno è indispensabile ', just as he is killed, on the bank of a canal in Venice one cold grey morning, by the fascists), *Terre d'Espagne, Salvatore Giuliano* – all these are titles which keep coming back to my mind, my eyes, my heart, my lungs. The occasional gust of fresh air I got from them were stolen from the countryside in those evil-smelling cinemas.

Knowledge, unfortunately, does not thrive on fresh air, sexy girls and clear water. What use is an emotional thrill when you are trying to work out a theory? All this wealth of sentiment, sold wholesale and for hard cash, was in danger of weakening us and turning us away from our purpose. We had to resist. After all, we were for the most part philosophers – in other words by profession we were enemies of innocence and the imagination. Though we went to the cinema like everyone else, though we read novels like so many other people, we also took courses in epistemology and the history of science in the École Normale at the Sorbonne, and we knew Spinoza personally. And this, whether we liked it or not, set us apart. In the genus 'French Youth', it was this that was our specific difference, a painful privilege we were forced into assuming. Since Bachelard was still the supreme master, we learnt among other things that scientific truth, which is the prime concern of the best people, is simply an ascent to the infinite, with successive pauses enabling one to see ever more clearly the distance one has come. Or alternatively, it is a series of battles between outward appearances, images and the force of habit on the one side, and one's fragile working concepts on the other. All the rules of battle are broken, and the battle itself never ends.

We also learnt, for we were good pupils, that the sirens of ideological error are always singing, on the cinema screen, in novels and in the street, and that few scholars are wise enough to close their ears fully to them. So, to save us from ourselves, we were taught to mistrust our own credulity and our enthusiasms, and to lay in a supply of ear-plugs as a protection. Actually the false glitter of 'the immediate' drew from some of our number such hatred and scorn that it seemed as though they had some kind of bone to pick with it, as if they had somehow had a quarrel with their own bodies. The rest of us, more vulnerable to love and probably less concerned with truth, merely became more circumspect. Though we did not break all our old links with literature, the theatre and the cinema, we resolved to be on our guard, and not let our feelings get the better of us. Alternatively, our aesthetic sense became more demanding. Beauty that has yielded is no longer beautiful; we wanted her to remain clothed and reserved, and certainly not provocative. Victor Hugo, Beethoven and Delacroix were like so many prostitutes to be enjoyed on Saturday night, but driven out of our heads afterwards with a little philosophy. Did the romantic period lend itself to vulgarity, or is it something we return to as we grow older? As we were barely over twenty, we remained halfway, with the contemporaries of our grandfathers – Ravel, Mallarmé, Bonnard. They were just what we wanted: our pleasures had to be a little high-brow, but not too much so. There was no reason why books and pictures should not provide a measure of enjoyment. Violence and pleasure must be interwoven, must as it were brush past one another, but never actually meet. Thus there seemed to us nothing to be ashamed of in actually enjoying the work of the critical approach which, with a studied leisureliness, took possession of its object and laid it bare. Or rather, perhaps, tore it apart. We could not bear the montages we could not see, the whole apparatus of connecting, joining, combining, scanning, derivations – the whole hidden way in which a work was put together. In one critical sentence, the most perfect flesh-and-blood women could be turned into plastic dolls; we played with their moving parts, and took them to pieces to reassemble them into monstrosities. That was how we proved our love for them, our pure, intellectual love.

Such a long-drawn-out battle against the demons of the heavens calls for a combination of astuteness and inflexibility that is beyond most young men. It is work for archangels – St Michael hurling down Lucifer. For a mere student there must be an apprenticeship, and it lasts for years. We had the years – four or five – ahead of us, to spend in a cloister designed for that very thing, whose entrance qualifications were so high that only the best Greek scholars could fulfil them. We had learnt our Greek, and they let us into the École Normale with our suitcases. For the first few months all was idyllic: it was autumn; the trees in the quadrangle were a magnificent gold; and no longer were school-masters watching our every move. The newcomer in particular relishes the strange sensation of having ended one life, and beginning at last a new and ' real ' one, a curious mixture of security and the unknown. But all too soon winter comes, and with it tedium. It is just that tedium, if he can manage to make the best of it, making it a daily practice and almost a moral virtue, which will be what will carry our newcomer through to wisdom, to a good degree, to a desirable job in a provincial college, and with a little luck, to being resigned to his lot. If he pushes himself harder, and works for a teaching qualification in philosophy, he will set about purifying the cultural system of his time, getting rid of its apparent errors, its deceptive inconsistencies, its distorted reflections. Such an undertaking can only succeed if he himself is prepared to leave behind all worldly vanity, and abandon the superficial for good. It is a matter of self-imposed abnegation, but let me make it clear that the abnegation I refer to is intellectual. Material and moral self-denial was for others! In our Hermitage we still ate like gourmets, went to the best tailors, and tinkered about with our little hire-purchase cars. With plenty of notice, we had time to use gentlemanly intrigue to get the pleasantest teaching jobs, by pay-ing court to the people who mattered at the Sorbonne and else-where – for even at the University a career does not just happen of itself. Our ascesis was of the mind: some worked at it from their second year, and in their striving for a formalized dissertation without flaw or deception of any kind, they became wholly immersed in Wittgenstein, Gödel and symbolic logic. There were others who wanted to ponder on the ambiguous autonomy of literary symbolism, and made their retreat far sooner to the stony deserts, taking as their guides and companions those great recluses of the written word, Char, Roussel, Michaux, Artaud, Ponge, Ezra Pound. On that thin strip of sand where the sunlight is blinding, those whose courage did not fail went off to explore; and they re-discovered or discovered metonymy, the outlines of the unconscious, the difficult paths of the significant.

The more timid, of whom I was one, hung back, and slowed down. We moved cumbersomely and were ashamed of the fact. It was hard to distinguish between what had too little meaning and what had too much – they looked just the same – and we were afraid of being lured by mirages or of basing our work on a mistaken idea. We also learnt to wonder whether what appeared ridiculous was really so. The richest meanings can be revealed in trivialities, and it is a commonplace that you can identify the truth by the trouble it takes to conceal itself. We thus grew rather attached to anything that looked really pathetic and derisory. Like people searching for treasure on the sea-floor, we set about fishing about in the backs of bookshops for all kinds of authors of small repute, tiny precious stones seen by the common run of people as mere pebbles, but enchanting to us because we could sense their hard work and discipline. Or, more simply, the hand of the craftsman. I must admit that I have long forgotten both authors and titles, but I do remember a kind of cult of craftsmanship for its own sake to which we all became more or less unconsciously addicted – as philosophically weighted as the belief in 'art for art's sake' which had fooled a previous generation.

As for contemporary prose, what we liked were rounded and polished works, as disturbingly smooth as glass balls with nothing you can get a grip on; our model was the short stories of Jorge Luis Borges. These perfectly constructed jewels provided us with double bases for discovery – their facets to harmonize, and their chiaroscuro to illuminate. Our discipline as professional exegetes thus paralleled that of those who actually created new forms, so that the two disciplines became one, and we could identify with them. The scrupulous ambiguity of their style demanded scrupulous scholars to interpret it – they needed *us*. We were suddenly more important. No longer mere commentators, we had become associate creators. If the public were to understand them, these philosophical writings, whether they knew it or not, needed philosophers of writing, and it then became hard to say which was the substance and which the shadow. Our age has seen critics of the arts turned into co-producers of the works they criticize. To feel of use is good; to consider oneself irreplaceable is overwhelming. For myself, I modestly glimpsed the possibility of appearing to advantage in the eyes of the experts, perhaps even of making my name once and for all. That would be a vocation in itself. It would be enough for me to remain forever in that austere world of philosophical exegesis, with one foot on each side of the line which is coming less and less – only by a ray of light, we used to say – to divide ideologues from imaginative writers. In the absence of one's own brilliant novel, one could do very well with a study on Gombrowicz – or so I thought. For that would be even more pointless.

Surely, now that we had read so much, it was our turn to start writing? A good reader is an unconscious writer. As professional readers we were not unaware of that axiom of all dying cultures, if only because we had grown up in that palace of mirrors which is Literature as taught in our schools. A discriminating reading public was waiting for us to come out, and to hear from our own mouths what splendours had been reflected in our critical spirits, and what marvellous creatures the Great Writers had become when subjected to our critical gaze. Certainly, since we were very young, our minds had been busy parading up and down among the works of other people; we were past masters at taking examinations in textual criticism, that keystone of all literary competitions. The moment had come for us as professionals to satisfy the curiosity of the amateurs; we must no longer leave them wondering.

The best thing of course would have been to create – novels, poems, film scripts. But since there is really no such thing as creating, since even the most original of fiction could still be accused of defiance or reaction or plagiarism, there could be nothing humiliating in dedicating oneself to literary or theoretical criticism, or both; with the added advantage that the basic stuff we would be working with was already there, in inexhaustible quantities, in the libraries. But whether we chose to prove ourselves by criticism or original work, the journey was still the same: the books already published by others, and read by us, would grow in our heads like seeds, and then tiny shoots, that must sooner or later flower into our own splendidly written pages. We would produce them in published form, and they, in their turn, would be read by others, and sow seeds in their heads, and so on *ad infinitum*. This parthenogenesis of the products of the mind suited us admirably. It was the only thing that gave us the moral force to overcome the panic that threatened to engulf us as we roved through the library of the college, with its endless shadowy rooms full of temptations, with the step-ladders and the catalogues, and smelling deliciously of polished wood and beeswax. We would go in looking for a Plato; we would come back with the history of the steam engine, the origins of Hinduism, Paracelsus, a handbook of phrenology – everything but Plato! And, oh, the agonies we suffered: the dizzying prospect of trying to touch and smell and leaf through everything, the fury at not being able to get ourselves properly organized, the irritation of moving uncertainly from shelf to shelf, the despair at the thought of trying hopelessly to dig over so much ground; and yet perhaps in spite of it all, the special joy of the farmer surveying the land that is his own. We would spend whole days in this way, distracted by far too many interests, squatting by the shelves, bent double in the half-light of the rooms, craning our necks on the ladders. But after the season of discomfort, of lumbago and cricks in the neck, there would be the joyous harvest time. And the fruits we gathered would be richer even than the promise in the seeds. For such Utopias were something we needed. We *had* to believe that literary expression would be self-reproducing, a pure and self-sufficient process, an eternal germination and flowering, for we hoped to be born of it in our turn. Sick, perhaps, of being anyone's son, of owing our being to an accident which one night long ago brought together two people who may even have been strangers, we intended to be born by our own decision, in our own right, to come to life, literally, by our pens. The children of our works. And what other work could we do but put pen to paper? This virtually automatic decision to write had no connection with the vocation of a writer – ours was to be a forger's job: we wanted to make our own copy of the act of our birth. We didn't know what to write in those forgeries; all we knew was that they would be the only things in which we could bear to recognize ourselves, all we could present as our own to those who would come to that library after us. It was a moralistic and erroneous aestheticism; we thought we could take root wherever we liked, deriving everything from the literature that was our earth.

I don't want to exaggerate. We did enjoy ourselves from time to time in our desert. We went to the music hall, for instance. No form of craftsmanship was to be despised. We went to the Olympia several times to hear Marlene Dietrich singing *The Blue Angel*. We might sit in the stalls or the balcony, but however much we moved about, she was always the same. The planned monotony of her movements, her voice by turns gravelly and clear, dignified and sexy, the precision with which she fulfilled her role and our expectations had a touch of Brecht about it which fascinated us. Some preferred Juliette Greco, but the ecstasy was the same. The quiet lighting, the economy of movement, the bare stage, everything indicated the endless rehearsals, the rigorous training, the total physical control. Not a shadow was left to chance – it was craftsmanship at its highest. Marlene and Greco were our worldly big sisters who had strayed onto the boulevard, robed in sequins and lights, untouchable, chastely glittering – for the brightness of the footlights covered them as completely as any clothes. They had created perfection in a style of their own, and its shape was determined for ever. It was final and frozen. We used to come out overwhelmed and having learnt much, and we hurried back up to the heights of our Pantheon to meditate on the lesson. Close by, under archways, sirens with warm and responsive bodies were luring away unwary mortals. It was unwise to spend much time on the boulevards, even just for a drink.

At about the same time, in contrast with this, an old friend of Boris Vian, a great writer to his own misfortune, laid before us confessions that were decidedly over-frank. He spoke of the bitterness of broken friendships, the grief of a complicated period which distorted justice and blurred the faces of fighters. He reawakened in us our lost sense of violence to prepare us against the cunning of the oppressors and help us not to be duped by it. He told of his own lapses, so that we should not commit the same ones: people who have done well in life always continue to blame themselves for their failures. But sadly enough his outbursts had a warmth of which we were suspicious, and to several of us such unseemly out-spokenness was most disconcerting. The less self-righteous among us pursed our lips. It was written as a first effort, without method, and obviously dictated by feeling – in short, it was subjective and histrionic in the extreme. But what was the use of being angry, if the subjectivity itself were a form of histrionics, a benign tumour on scholarship, as we then saw it to be? The idolator was driven out of our desert. Sartre was definitely not one of us.

‘ Us ’ could still be counted on the fingers of one hand. And in truth, we used to write people off most forcefully. But there was no guarantee that a given author we had proscribed would not slip back surreptitiously, and find his way back to our hearts and our Pantheon without our noticing. Both indeed were virtually empty, while the banished were legion. And for what they were worth, our decrees still remained a matter of opinion, with nothing very solid to legitimize them. It was at that point that a fine philosopher who was guiding our steps as students, and had intro-duced us to Karl Marx, gave us the entrée to the kingdom he was himself exploring, that of theoretical rigour and dialectical materialism, as a theory of general praxis; he shared everything with us, and handed over to us his own discoveries to work on. We jumped into this Promised Land with both feet. We had been floundering around for so long that we had barely crossed the threshold when we felt utterly at home, as much at ease as our guide if not more so; in fact we almost banished him for being over-timid. Our group had found a good home. Here ended our rather cursory quest. Theoreticians have no history, and successful discipline has only the history of its own fruits. From now on, it was left to our concepts to increase and multiply in peace. We knew there would be time. That was something pre-determined.

So there we were – safe, and solid and indeed ennobled, but not overwhelmed. This new foundation did not demand any change in our way of life; we had but to build upon the habits we had already formed – habits which it supported. So we received our titles of honour without blinking. Who could ask for more? We had found a work of genuine transformation, and one which could be done at home or in the library; it was hard work, but all it required was material we already had in plenty, our family inheritance, the ideologies of the bourgeoisie; enough self-discipline to achieve one production; and though that production would have its individual laws, it would provide a pattern which could be used for all other possible productions. In short, what came to be called 'theoretical praxis' caught us at just the right moment. Obviously it also came to fulfil the role of an ideology: it concealed our conflicts by justifying them, making them appear inevitable and valuable. And this 'ideological' use we made of 'theory' was in return of service to theoretical praxis, enabling us to make positive use of our weaknesses and really learn from them. Those weaknesses, isolation and self-complacency, are calamities which affect anyone who lives cut off from the mainstream of life, and especially from politics and economics. All very fine: theory draws its effectiveness from its rigorousness, and its rigorousness is effective because it separates 'development in reality' from 'development in thought', the 'operation of society' from the 'operation of knowledge'. In other words, all we had to do to become good theoreticians was to be lazy bastards. In fact, as some of the richest beneficiaries of a class society, we were better placed than anyone to develop revolutionary theory, or at least to preserve it from attack by bourgeois ideologies. In countries which are trying to build a socialist society, students are obliged to spend a good part of the year doing productive work in farms or factories. They are concerned at least to know what life is like for those who produce material goods, and it makes them more modest if less erudite, more aware though perhaps less scholarly. But we had been accustomed from our earliest years to see intellectual work as something quite apart from productive work, and to consider this social division as the obverse of an inevitable technical division of labour. We knew from our reading that capitalism sanctioned and reinforced that division, but we were anxious to make the best of things. What, we would say, can you do in any situation but come to terms with it? We tried to formulate it differently: all work was production, and our intellectual work would be production like any other and should be taken just as seriously. We would produce theoretical concepts just as other people produced forks or cabbages, and we would do it all the better for not having had to plant or cut or even cook the cabbages, but only eat them.

Besides, our rigorousness provided us with an excellent intellectual apprenticeship. It can be of use in any and every situation; I have tried to make use of it since, in other less rarefied spheres. In our then situation, it seems to me that our exclusive preoccupation with theory was, even so, not wholly without danger, even though only extrinsically, in that it provided us with alibis. By hastening to define our philosophical activity as practical work like any other, we believed ourselves absolved from other forms of work. Since theoretical work could be taken as a model for all other work – at least a model of intelligibility – and since that was the work we did, it put us once again back on a pedestal, and made us arbiters of custom, of ideas, and of revolutions, the omniscient inspectors of the weights and measures of the world. The day Marxist theory was purged of its ideological waste matter and restored to itself as a highly polished tool of knowledge, the revolution would be halfway to success, or merely in need of completion. Though even the least wise of us would have denied holding any such crude notion, it was none the less this that dictated our assurance that we could restore the badly compromised course of the socialist revolution, with the help of our ideas, working away among themselves in a kind of retort, rather as we were inside the four walls of our *thurnes*.

I am wrong, of course. Such assertions are too outrageous to be true. The fact is that I have left what little philosophy I had in the guardroom, together with my belt and my shoe-laces, and what I have suffered has faded my intellectual memory as it whitens some people's hair. But I do not think I am wrong in calling attention, not to the details of a system, but to the moral justifications we wrote into it which were not of its nature but simply our error. Concepts that are genuinely theoretical – that is fitted to their object and providing an effective and measured mastery of it –

become blind and useless when they descend to the details of experience. Immediately and at ground level, therefore, everything was allowed without compromising our flights of theory. Having disqualified 'experience' we could breathe easily. It was a very lax kind of rigorousness; restricted to the written word, it left us free to do what we wished in every other sphere. In fact, we knew almost everything about Marxism and Leninism except the essential: that its counterpart, communism, is also an ethic. Its theory is not complete, for it cannot be and never will be. It is not to be found written down anywhere, except in silly little catechisms which have about as much in common with that ethic as a brothel with love. And we had not really come up against it, except to dismiss it into the realms of 'ideology' as one of the bits of troublesome litter lying along the paths of Theory. In effect, once having taken theory abroad, it was for each of us to guide his own boat, and how could we know how to do that, having never been anywhere near the sea? From the shelter of our scholarly bay, away from the wind and the heavy seas outside, we arranged the comfortable conditions we needed to do our regular work, with no particular wish to meet or get to know people who shared neither our material standard of living, nor the social status which we felt to be our natural right. Surely it did not matter. Such minor lacunae would hardly show up in the accounts, except as the small change of our intellectual labours. Must one live as a bourgeois to think as a Marxist? It is said that some comforts are uncomfortable to have acquired, rendered uneasy by a bad conscience. We suffered no such bourgeois disease; our consciences were bursting with health.

Watch out: a shockingly petty bourgeois concept of what is 'bourgeois' looks like coming to light here. But this is not the moment to analyse it. It may be childish to judge intellectual work by the insulated environment it demands rather than the use it makes of it – its results. Children talk like that about generals: they consider them despicable for sending their troops to die without ever risking their own lives, forgetting that without them there wouldn't be any battles or any armies at all. The theoreticians we wanted to be were rather the same – staff officers directing battles from the depths of their bomb shelters, with a finger on the map. We had an excuse of course. We were not at war, and we sent no one out to die – only to read *Capital*. As Marxists, we were not even aware that communists are still the most mortal of all men. And besides, we weren't wrong to want to shut ourselves up in comfort. No one can do any thinking in a crowd or in a high wind, and I have found to my cost what precarious balance of the stomach, nerves and ears – food, sleep and silence – is needed to support even the healthiest intellectual workers. The miracles of the brain are brought about by very commonplace means. Should only one of these conditions be lacking for long enough, one starts to be able to think only of that and of nothing else. I have suffered a great deal from hunger; enough to feel cut down to size as an ex-intellectual more or less for good. If you are hungry, you can finally think of nothing but your hunger, with the anxious and self-involved lassitude that makes you have to think for five minutes before taking three steps – so that you decide with a certain selfish cunning that it would be unwise to stand up and get water for a sick comrade – that corrodes your attentiveness, makes it seem daily more justifiable to care about nothing, closes your eyes, prevents you even from reading.

In my case it did not matter much. But consider a major intellectual like Ramón,[1] for instance, who has pushed intellectual rigour to the point of freely and permanently denying himself the balance it demands. So much so that he could no longer take advantage of the respite of a day's halt on a march or during fighting. Sitting on his hammock, with a book on economics in his hand, I can see Ramón, teeth clenched, fighting the heat, the mosquitoes, torpor of mind and body, after several days with no more than his morning's black coffee. And that for days, months and years. I have known him over one page all day, reading and re-reading words he could not take in, but refusing to admit defeat. Though he had written an economics textbook, he had chosen to live in that jungle 'where I have been waiting for the last six

1. Ramón was the pseudonym of Commandant Guevara.

months to study a book you can find in any local bookshop in a big town, a book I need to finish a chapter of my own. Ten years! I want ten years of peace and quiet after this war is over so as to work out and set down what really matters . . .' Yet, in spite of everything, he scrambled up cliffs and crossed rivers, where men before him had yielded to exhaustion and been swept away by the current; and all this with a whole library on his back, which his comrades gradually managed to insist on sharing, to lighten his load. A French language text, a novel, a collection of poems, and a book of mathematics can amount to a fearful load when added to the ammunition-clips, the bags of rice and sugar, the serum, the bottle of oil, and so on. Even when ill, after losing well over forty pounds, he refused to leave anything out, but wrapped it all up, fastened his pack with ropes to keep everything together, knelt down to get his arms through the straps, and would manage after two or three attempts to stand up, with his back hurting enough to make him grimace with anger. He was the last to sit down when they arrived somewhere, the first ready to leave. And he always stayed in the front as an example. Torn by the undergrowth, slipping about in the mud with the weight of his sack beyond his control, falling over and swearing as he got up again, and going on in silence. Even when so ill, so thin; and he did it for days, for months, for years.

But that is a sad story, and this is not the place for it; no one who has heard it will soon forget it, that underground story of a different sort of rigour which puts ours, all of ours, to shame. It may not be the kind of rigour that will produce a rigorous dissertation. It involves too great a danger of death to be certain of any such happy ending. I did not mean to say anything about this story, which other people will write fully one day, but it has come up none the less, because I keep thinking of all those who can at least write, as I can, at this moment, and who basically have nothing to communicate, and of those who cannot write and yet have so much to tell us. I keep thinking too of all those inactive people who get three thousand calories a day which they do not need, and of those who need them so badly (for their sakes and ours) as they sweat and stagger under packs that they can hardly carry and yet every item in which is vital, and I think how only half of what the others eat would do them very nicely. People should be moved around, roles should be reversed, and then human energies will be working properly. If only the fighting men could briefly be removed from combat and sent into the bomb-shelters of the theoreticians, while the generals replaced them for a moment on the field of battle!

But, let us get back to our rather more pleasant theme of over-confident young men.

It was at about the same time that Algeria achieved inde-pendence that France achieved a certain stability, and we achieved intellectual coherence. Oddly enough our cohesion as a group suffered. It was of course the moment when the first rifts would have occurred among us in any case, for we were becoming adults. The 'epistemological gap' dividing adequate from inadequate knowledge had already split the world quite decisively into two. The division coincided almost exactly with the line of walls and railings separating our hermitage – the École Normale – from the rest of society, with the numbers of 'misfits' on both sides being about equal. To sort out our confused ideas, we were beginning to cultivate a kind of distinction of mind which comes dangerously near to snobbishness pure and simple. The same sense of intel-lectual hierarchies which from the first established an unbridgeable gulf between ourselves and the non-initiated, was now beginning to affect our own relationships. Imperceptible chinks already there began to grow wider; it may have been as much a matter of temperament as of ability, with the more hard-working going ahead, while the slower remained dreaming. Gradually there came to be masters and vassals within our own caste. Subtle distances came to be recognized, to which some people were forced to become resigned, while others actively fostered them. As for out-siders who persisted in hanging around us, we came to view them from our heights on a kind of vertical scale, ranging down from esteem, or even a certain indulgent familiarity, to simply ignoring their existence, according to the rung on the ladder of knowledge occupied by each one; it was a somewhat rigid Spinoza-style placing, which had the advantage of creating differences of status or category, not merely among the ideas, but also among those who held the ideas – to say nothing of the rest of mankind. And when, from the heights of the 'steep footpaths of science', we would stop for a moment to look down, it was not without a certain pleasure that we saw the line of climbers panting behind us, unfortunates held back by the weight of their own chatter and idleness. We did not look down, I need hardly say, with any thought of going to their assistance, but only to note how far we had come and to appreciate our own advance as compared with theirs. They thought we despised them. Yet it was hardly our fault that we were perched so much higher. We did indeed have a certain modest pride. The metaphysicians were marked by their petulance and trenchancy. We, since we had learnt from the positive sciences that to ask a question correctly brings you halfway to answering it, were marked by our reserve and our insistence on verbal precision. In our dissertations we relished a careful choice of words, lengthy opening remarks, and a reluctance to conclude; in our dress, the discreet elegance of a well-cut jacket; in our behaviour, an unobtrusive manner, a quiet voice, and only the occasional gesture. In the Goethean idiom still in fashion at the beginning of the century, the old-style socialists who had preceded us in this school could have predicted of us: 'They will be men of order rather than justice.' We should have been much amused by such a naïve description – without realizing that in their terms what they were saying was absolutely true. We were on good terms with the existing order, and felt that our reward was not to be long in coming.

Our very rigorousness raised walls amongst us, rather like those put up by landowners along country roads to set their private property apart. Few friendships came into being in this situation, and many were broken up, often without the friends themselves realizing what was happening, and even in spite of their wishes. They could not understand the barriers of silence which were beginning to rise up around them. It was not their fault, but the fault of their ideas, whose universal application had to be forged in secret. Once worked out, those ideas would be open to everyone. But to incubate them called for well-heated *thurnes*, locked doors, and furtive conversation, almost in code. One could so easily catch cold – or have one's ideas stolen! One young Marxist once made the mistake of telling another Marxist friend of his about the work he was doing. In the few steps he took down one of those draughty corridors where any meeting inevitably involved one in *some* conversation, he let one or two, still incomplete, concepts slip out, and the other unconsciously snapped them up, and reproduced them some time later as his own. Indeed he may well have worked them out for himself, but in other words. The originator considered that he had been robbed and complained loud and long; the plagiarist disagreed; witnesses were summoned. There was a great to-do, with a promising concept at issue, and the two friends broke up forever. It was a heavy price to pay, but as far as we were concerned it was the law of the land.

We reached that bitter stage when you discover that there is nothing to be gained and much to be lost by chatting to friends. We were amazed to find that we felt faintly annoyed if we met one another; the rites of friendship began to bear the weight of habit, to which we only submitted through indolence, and we would later regret the time we had wasted together. Each of us became involved in his budding career, his unformulated ambitions, his wife, his failures; each gradually withdrew into himself. We became polite and careful, stopping to think before making even the smallest joke, so defensive and cautious had we become. Our relationships with friends in different disciplines were the first to go. Then it came to be that those working in the *same* field began to be careful what they said, so as to avoid blunders, and spare other people's feelings. We used always to go out in a group, especially after dinner in the evening, to have coffee in a neighbouring bistro. It was a traditional way of preserving our friendships and proving how carefree we were. The sloth that comes with the digestive process is overcome better when several people digest in company, and we hastened the process with jokes and laughter. But now, between the taciturnity which had always been our stock-in-trade and an offensive refusal to speak at all, there gradually came into being an indeterminate middle way, marked by rather dour smiles. Everyone waited for someone else to be the first to speak. Someone would venture a sarcasm which would at once meet with disapproval; another would attack some recent work and be met with sarcasm. It became a vicious circle: we would all run after one another vainly trying to catch up. It was a dismal kind of hide and seek, but we could not cure it by letting ourselves fall into that kind of rough and rather vulgar camaraderie which made other boys of our age roar with laughter at the tables all round us. Their merriment, so painful to our ears, had so little content, it seemed – a few shared memories, a Saturday night's drinking, a visit to a brothel, a fight, a few hours in the cells.

This kind of amusement which filled the gaps in the lives of ordinary young men had never sullied ours. We were not even allowed to experience that animal side of human fraternity enjoyed by drinking companions, fellow-soldiers, people on day-trips to the country. We should have blushed to introduce any such trivialities into our world. Our mistresses or absence thereof, our families, our social blunders – all these had too little connection with Truth or with our studies to be worth talking about. There was no possible foothold for us on that ground of easy understanding, shared by all who let themselves be young, whatever their ideas or situations. The reason for this was that, having become scholars too soon and too easily, we had moved straight from childhood to intellectual maturity, and by-passed that age in between which we did not care to have brought to our notice. We did all that we could to pretend it did not exist. It is not an enviable lot to move straight from the front row of the classroom to the teacher's desk, without ever having larked about at the back, and seldom even played in the playground; but that was more or less what we had done. Though it may have earned us valuable time in the race for excellence and the search for truth, it had made us awkward and self-conscious for life. I am convinced that it was this forced abandonment of youth that was the major cause of all our inhibitions. We did not want to see our own weakness, so we were forced to suppress all youthfulness in ourselves and found it hard to tolerate in others. We were rather ashamed of being young at all, and yet fundamentally, we were ashamed of being ashamed.

Our café meetings, idle to the point of tedium, developed into silences broken by conventional exchanges, and ended without ever reaching any real conclusions. They left each of us with a sense of dissatisfaction with himself for having come, and with the others for having been there too. We would separate finally both relieved and irritated – relieved at having got rid of the others, irritated at having done it so ungracefully. With that uncomfortable sense of having said both too much and too little, of having left unsaid what should have been said, and having said what should not have been said, a combination of chagrin and regret which seems to me to come upon all friends at parting. Whether by chance or lack of experience or carelessness, some of us prematurely made fellow-students pregnant, and got married – thus having a good reason for cutting short these already pointless meetings.

At last came the final year; summer with all the exams, and then the unexpected appointments in provincial universities, or abroad, or, for the lucky ones, in Paris. Promotion fell to us ripe from the sun, parcelled out by various examinations, cut into by holidays, a failed oral, a marriage, or temporarily delayed by a period of work in an underdeveloped country, or military service. Our last cup of coffee together. We were no longer really friends; to some extent we were now colleagues though we didn't fully recognize it; there were jokes, handshakes all round, a reluctance to look one another straight in the eye. We would, of course, spend holidays together, we would write to one another, we would meet again next year – all so many empty promises, kindly lies. Each one of us colluded in the general betrayal, agreeing noisily while knowing in our heart of hearts that we were separating for good. Once set in the grooves of a career, what escape could there be, what with family obligations, papers to mark, the overwork that falls to the lot of every teacher, the sheer distances separating us? We knew in advance that it was hopeless. In future our only correspondence would be by thesis, by article, through the columns of specialist journals. We should get printer's ink to say – and leave unsaid – the words that, meeting face to face, seemed to fail us.

And so they vanished, our former comrades and friends, to the four corners of Knowledge, becoming almost like strangers despite the years spent together. Linguistics, economics, modern logic, psychoanalysis, sociology, the history of mathematics, epistemology, the new criticism – all these hungry monsters dragged away their prey, leaving no trace behind. We were never to see them again: specialist studies consume people in secret. Knowledge clanged its doors upon a lot of adolescents: in fifty years' time – for its victims are long-lived – those doors would open to give us back their bones, gleaming and licked clean, consisting of perhaps four or five major works, a reference in a textbook, a handful of faithful disciples. (It is this last bequest to posterity that stands up best.)

Most of us were communists, by which I mean members of the Communist Party and faithful readers of its press. We actually took it in turns, once a week, to stick up a copy of *L'Humanité* on the wall opposite, in defiance of all the rules: nor did we attach the regulation stamp. From us, who were so many feudal apprentices, this might smack of affectation. There was something a little incongruous in these stern cavaliers of Knowledge, moving stiffly in their breast-plates of Pure Concept, going down into the street with their glue-pots. Yet this incongruity was but the natural result of everything else. Some of us, though in fact very few, were communists by family tradition. They got on so well with their fathers, and still lived in such sweet dreams that it would have been cruel to disturb them. For the majority, it was simply a glorious chance that had brought us into contact with the philosophy teacher who guided our work and our reading. He tactfully gave us the chance of working with him, in such a way that we did not realize that it was he who actually did the work, that he was working for us.

We knew he was a communist, and under his influence, though without telling him, we became so too. But with him it was a whole-hearted conviction, as could be seen not only from his written works, but from the affection and generosity with which he guided our steps in that direction. For what his students saw as his personal qualities were in fact those of every activist. In most cases, perhaps all, this was a misconception which gradually faded away of its own accord. Since it was Marx who had first given them the keys to ' theoretical production ', they made the mistake in all good faith of believing that to become a Marxist theoretician obliged one to become a communist. So they reluctantly paid their dues, rather ashamed of thus straying from the straight and narrow path, but they soon returned to it. No amount of *noblesse* could oblige them thus to rub shoulders with the proletariat. And in fact the working-class Party was not specially anxious to have us either. It was never suggested that we meet or become friends with comrades from a background different from our own; I think it was felt preferable to leave the initiative to us, and we had neither the means nor the wish to take it. In any case, such populism would have seemed to us misplaced. Had we been taken at our word, we would have been in something of a quandary. We hardly knew even where to find the workers, and in any case, what would have been the use? So we studied away in our corridors, our *thurnes*, our local cafés. It was a bit dull, but at least it insured us against embarrassing encounters of any kind.

For, in fact, we were only really at ease with Marx's writings, and the complete works of Lenin whose twenty-odd volumes, with their red bindings and pale green jackets, lined our shelves. Those we read, underlined, quoted, re-read. That precise and cumbersome style of Lenin's, with its well-structured framework, its unemotional and meaningful sentences – almost dull at times, avoiding any artificial whipping up of emotion, using so few images – established for us the norm for all possible political writing, and gave us a model to copy. We could barely conceive the possibility that other cultures, climates or temperaments might ever produce models of any other kind.

Occasionally there would be a diversion. We would dress in the correct way – a sweater with a few holes, corduroy trousers, old shoes – and go out, with our identity cards in our pockets, to join a demo, be hit with a stick or a rolled-up cape, stand silently by as someone was buried, march through the streets rhythmically shouting out our hatred of a fascism which had never done us any harm. Tortures, ambushes, wounded generals, escapes, guerrilla fighting, rape, genocide: what was happening in Algeria rocked the metropolis and the whole world watched. Every dog has his day, every country its war. We shouted along the boulevards – though with dignity – 'Free Ben Bella!', and 'OAS murderers!' But the police could hit hard, and several of our friends had to be taken to hospital. In spite of everything, these joyless diversions excited us and we felt good afterwards. We would come away from them stunned, exalted, talking of nothing else for several days. They were evidence that we too were fighting, that we were militant; evidence, too, that times were hard.

Apart from these slight risks, it cost little to call oneself a communist. Five new francs a month, if I remember rightly, and one or two meetings a week at which we only met each other, but formally this time, with fierce argument over matters of procedure and agenda. Those punctilious preliminaries used up our energy and our bitterness, so that when the time came to make decisions, we would be ready to decide anything, and leave the session with all its acrimony exhausted, putting off until the following week any serious discussion of the statement produced, which had satisfied no one. And so it went on. These debates which we were too scrupulous ever to bring to a head, seldom led anywhere, because there was very little to discuss, and what there was always remained in the family.

What disturbed us rather more was reading newspapers and reviews, for we then had to stop splitting hairs and take up a definite position. But the apparent inanity of some of the editorials, and the apparent complacency we found in some of the articles, did not disturb us overmuch. They certainly irritated some militants who were more alive than we to possible repercussions from the outside world, but we had all seen through other and cleverer traps, and saw these as mere play-acting. The snares of the immediate had not been able to deceive *us* for a very long time. But unfortunately since these publications were made public, they would lie about on tables, on radiators, in the hall. Anyone could look at them, and there was always a sympathizer naive enough to take them at face value, and embarrass us with questions about peaceful coexistence, imports of Canadian corn, or the new-style Democracy. The poor things were not in the secret as we were: we of course knew that these stereotypes were mere cover-ups; we had learnt how to read between the lines, to understand why an adjective was omitted or a comma put in unexpectedly – or even, in moments of despair, simply to insert it ourselves, to gain a little time. As a result of our detailed reading of Lenin under Figuères or Garaudy, we soon became adept at such exercises in simultaneous translation, and in the end could digest in a matter of minutes even those fantasies most devoid of our beloved theoretical rigour – with a certain pitying scorn for the petty bourgeois, our less skilled companions who were left totally baffled. But most of us, I imagine, must ultimately have recognized our own illogicality.

Then too we had our knightly vigil on the eve of elections, when we would go down to the local hall and come close to those distant oracles whose newspaper messages we de-coded every morning, actually attaching a face to the famous name, or putting a less well-known name to a better-known face. There they were in a row, in order of age and importance, under the red hangings on the stage, sitting behind a long table, also swathed in red. In the hurly-burly of the crowded hall, we would get there too late to find seats and those who had arrived early enough were beginning to be impatient. We pointed out the leaders, talking over their various names and merits, proud of being able to recognize some, pleased to get to know the others. The more our representatives looked like members of the lower middle class, the better we liked it – for it proved that they were nothing of the kind. Everything proved us right: their rayon ties, their paunches, their jolly smiles, the rhythmic rumbling of their speech, full of good sense and signifying nothing. From old sepia photographs the Bolsheviks of legend looked down upon us from the beginning of the century, like so many comfortable stockbrokers in their bowler hats, stiff collars and frock-coats. Everything we knew of them, their very names, belied their appearance. For young people lacking both experience and theory, and consequently talkative and unstable, to be more attracted by the ostentatious austerity of the Chinese, standing like statues in their tunics, or by the relaxation of the Cubans, never still and caring nothing for ceremony, seemed to be in the order of things; it confirmed us in our wisdom, and increased our support for the officials lined up on the stage in front of us. They had risked their future in 1936, their lives in the Resistance, their parliamentary immunity in the strikes and conflicts of the post-war period, without making any display, and were adapting to the new situation with just the same dedication. We thought of all this as we watched them on the stage, and felt deeply moved. Besides, every one of us knew that the bonfires of *gauchisme* are made up of straw and cannot last. But this gentle fire which our leaders kept going without any of those flashing but useless sparks had survived so many trials in the past that it was nowhere near going out. Smouldering at its base was a working-class hardness, obstinate and unwearying, the unspoken will of the people, a future of action rather than words.

Merely to see the hall and the excited crowd was reward enough for our fidelity to the Party. As we came in, we were certainly disconcerted by the shoving on the stairs, the shouting, the crowd, the smell, the stamping in the aisles. It is always like that at first. It is a matter of atmosphere. One cannot feel immediately at ease at such a meeting, any more than one does if one comes, hungry and thirsty, upon a cheerful party of revellers. But, bit by bit, as we stood shoulder to shoulder, we caught the audience's enthusiasm. As we relaxed, our reservations were swept away in waves of shouting, and a sense of need to become part of what was going on around us took possession of us. We attended not so much to the speeches, which we already knew practically by heart, but to the way the crowd listened to them. A burst of applause broke the silence of the listeners, and we too applauded for sheer joy, till our hands smarted, and the whole hall followed us in shouting out the appropriate slogan, clapping in time to the words. Our more disciplined neighbours were forced to reprove us good-humouredly for our ill-timed interruptions. And when the speech ended to the accompaniments of stamping and shouts of approval, as the speaker returned to his seat with his notes under his arm, we let ourselves go completely and joined in the uproar. And as we shouted, we could almost see ourselves alongside the shirt-sleeved workers, in the front line, our hair flying in the wind, bullets bursting all round us, ready to take the red flag from the hands of a dying comrade as he made one supreme effort to pass it across, advancing undeterred under fire, our shirts torn, our eyes blazing, against the terrified bourgeoisie – correctly-dressed bankers, monocled officers and so on – fleeing before us in confusion down the Boulevard St Germain.

We could, of course, abandon ourselves freely to such childish fantasies quite safely in a legally rented hall with good thick walls and our neighbours all on our side. But finally the last speaker – the most applauded and least original of all – had finished his peroration; victory was certain, the unity of all republicans assured, we had abolished the power of the individual once and for all, and everyone in the hall was standing to applaud, cheering and booing, uttering random demands and singing snatches of the Internationale. This warm and cathartic experience was over. We got as far as the exits, utterly at one with the crowd and the shouting, happy to be part of it all, positively enjoying the jostling. Our ears still rang with the final tirade, and we hummed the Internationale or the 'Young Guard' as we went down the stairs, throwing coins generously into the collection.

Outside, on the pavement, in front of their dark blue police vans, cordons of uniformed police watched us go by with an absent gaze. The forces of order they were, but what they actually aroused in us was a vague desire for *dis*order, and we stayed there, in random bunches, moving from group to group rather than going away, stamping our feet, waiting for we didn't know what reaction, some unforeseen brush, some altercation, which would give us an excuse to start singing, or to march somewhere – anywhere. We walked back and forth in front of these rows of helmets and batons, staring provocatively with our noses in the air, like rebels champing at the bit – as though these sleepy-looking *flics* had only our restraint to thank for not being torn to pieces on the spot. Yet somehow the singing died away, we sweated until our shirts stuck clammily to our backs, and gradually the crowd thinned as people went off to catch their last Métro. Nothing happened at all. We did not know who issued it, but an order that no one could have challenged or disobeyed passed among us 'to disperse in silence and do nothing if provoked'. Wise though we realized it to be, it was still irksome to have to pass the word on in a low voice to one's neighbour. Then, because there was nothing else to do, we went to the corner bar for a drink, with the silence of despair rather than of discipline, trying to think about something else and make the best of it. Our confrontation with the police would have to be put off till next time. And we went slowly back up our hill, in small groups, growing smaller as people turned off at each dark side street, barely speaking, not daring to look one another in the eye, suffering that uneasy mixture of shame and hope which can only be called a sense of the unfinished.

Life went on as usual, with all its usual reserve. One night was enough to make us forget what had happened. The next morning, we woke refreshed and alert, working better than before, our heads clear, our hearts easy. One's body needs the occasional convulsion, and one must give the body what it demands. Such convulsive experiences were like purges, cleansing us from time to time, a few times a year. You could describe them as part of our general keep-fit programme.

We went through the same hopes and the same betrayals when we came home late at night from the mass demonstrations on the boulevards, where despite the huge numbers, the bloodshed and the scuffles, there was never a real riot, and no power was overthrown. Within twenty-four hours the wounded had disappeared, and with them our anger; order took over again, even in our minds. Towards the end of the Algerian war, there was talk of a civil war. Thrilled and excited, we made a few preparations, spent one or two splendidly sleepless nights, and several days making wild speeches. But it never happened. Cause for congratulation, surely, and, dishonestly, we congratulated ourselves. Bit by bit we learnt to enjoy these experiences of disillusionment, which we found inwardly exciting, though outwardly we deplored them. We mistook them for our apprenticeship in political maturity, seeing them as stages in it. We turned all these minor battles we had lost into so many defeats of the class enemy – which certainly was not troubled by them at all, and indeed had everything to gain from our taking this particular path to maturity. And when one of us finally got tired of fighting the demon of irresponsibility within him, when he could no longer go on convincing himself, he would turn to attack those woolly left-wing moralists who were always excited, always ready to fall in love with the first revolution they met, as long as it was good and far away, preferably somewhere in the tropics. Strong in our knowledge of Lenin – we knew the passages about compromise almost by heart – it was easy enough for us to abuse their naïvety, and abusing them brought a certain relief to those of us who felt most insecure. *Our* revolution, or rather our restoration of democracy, would take place without upheavals, by imperceptible moves, with official receptions given by local authorities, compromises on matters of detail, electoral gains interspersed with withdrawals of candidates and molecular mass movements. After all, what could people like us, whose class instinct drew us to use as our weapons pointless impatience and abuse, what could we know of the conditions prevailing in the class struggle at its grass roots, of the possibilities and the chances? What experience had formed us? We heard the voice of experience from the mouths of our representatives, who never stopped appealing to its ambiguous lessons. It taught them to keep an eye on the future. For the moment we could sleep in peace, and if we suffered from insomnia, we must simply keep calm. For what reason I am not certain, but I imagine to avoid being entrapped by the deceits of tinsel and the confusions of the bourgeoisie, we ended up believing that nothing that glittered could ever really be gold.

What fools we were. It was we who were being naïve. We were wrong from the first. Where we should have let ourselves go, we were restrained. Where we should have been mistrustful, we trusted. We were misled by our own cleverness. If we got nowhere, we had only ourselves to blame. *Not* for having mistaken trickery for compromise, confusion for a situation of hopefulness, and our leaders for Bolsheviks. *Not* for having let ourselves be taken in by the voice of 'experience', that magic phrase for the innocent and the defeated. That pompous and measured voice only says what one asks it to say. Those characters we pointed out to one another at the *Mutualité* were certainly not Bolsheviks, but nor were they charlatans; they were well-meaning poor wretches who had been fighting a losing battle for twenty years, trying to save with one hand the goods they were selling off with the other. With France and Guy Mollet being what they were, they could probably not have done otherwise. There was no future for them in any case. And certainly no one else would have been willing to take on their job.

No. What appals me is those cloudy images which befogged our minds as we marched together behind a banner, or stamped on the floor behind closed doors. In those moments of exhilaration in which we lost our sense of solitude, we thought we were to some degree making history, contributing our little grain to the sands of time – whereas in fact we were using the small change of our fantasies to pay for our total lack of history (our only connection with it!). Again, it is all too easy to mistake a psychodrama for a fragment of an epic. Illusions of that kind produce a dependence in the patient, and that is where the real trouble starts. The withdrawal is all the more painful, when we have to learn to our cost – and almost against our will – what it was that our elders knew and kept to themselves, and why it was that we did not understand the meaning of their silence. That at all those moments when it is important to be a communist and remain one, to stand and stand firm, the man who has been carried away with enthusiasm at meetings, swept along with the excitement of unknown comrades, surrounded and supported by neighbours, suddenly finds himself alone, on the ground, perhaps left undressed in a bare room, with no public, no platform, no neighbours, no singing to join in, no support of any kind. If he sweats, it won't be because he is too hot. There are the *flics* with their cigarettes or knuckle-dusters; there is the revolver in your back, in some unknown district at about seven in the evening; there is the threat of third degree that might well end in death. There is the chance of apostasy – no one will see as you sign a statement in exchange for your freedom. You might be the one man who has to hide behind a stone to wait for an enemy patrol for two days and nights, with only a bit of boiled maize in his pocket, so as to defend a path through the forest. Or a time comes when you know you should put the heavy shovel, forgotten in a corner of the camping place, into your pack, and your knees are trembling with hunger, and since no one knows you have noticed it, it would be so easy to leave it behind. Times when there are no witnesses, no comrades with you. You have to sing under your breath without moving your lips, so as to fill up the silence with people, and make yourself feel that you are marching in a great crowd, without daring to move an inch.

These are so many commonplaces which everyone learns all over Europe in wartime, but they are not taught to us in times of peace, and we were lucky enough to grow up in peacetime, in the pleasant and fertile land of France. But that very luck unfortunately brings its own limitations. For no one even hinted to us that this era with its meetings and straightforward duties was an exceptional one, existing only in some places, a state of good fortune which might well come to be replaced by a state of siege. Since that time, other communists have taught me that 'to disperse in silence and do nothing if provoked' was certainly not a maxim to be handed on unthinkingly, and still less to be admired. It is a funeral chant which in recent times has accompanied the slaughter of people all over the world; small, unimportant nations, of course, in the eyes of the great States who have used such maxims not merely as pieces of wisdom, but as policies.

The same people have also taught me that, as a general rule, if you are ever forced to disperse, you must re-form at once behind the backs of the enemy, and that a provocation that meets with no response will inevitably be followed by another. I realize that such simple-minded people are trouble-makers. After all, they have one socialist revolution on their consciences already, and others on the way. They are bad men who give a bad example. And realists and politicians will not forgive them readily, for *they* do not live calmly; they do not read out prepared speeches; they are passionately anxious to carry conviction, and the future in their hands sounds like being hard work. But their warmth communicates itself: anyone who is with them for a time feels his blood stirring and his vision becoming keener, for it would seem that fire and perspicacity go hand in hand. You no longer fear deceptions: gold really does glitter. Appearances, our work, do not deceive. Leaders can be recognized a mile off by their whole bearing, traitors by their shifty looks, cowards by their softness – and, yes, revolutions do hurt. All the old clichés are true, and I shall hold on to them. Even if it is a bit late.

About the Author

<small>REGIS DEBRAY</small> was born in 1941 and educated at the Ecole Normale Supérieure, Paris. He has spent long periods in Cuba and elsewhere in Latin America, studying the various radical parties and movements and visiting guerrilla fronts where possible. On the basis of these experiences he wrote two long articles, "Le Castrisme: la longue marche de l'Amérique Latine," published in Sartre's review *Les Temps Modernes* in 1963, and "América Latina: algunos problemas de estrategia revolucionaria" in 1965; these articles established Debray's reputation. In 1966 he took up a chair in philosophy at the University of Havana. He was given access to numerous unpublished documents, spoke with participants in the Cuban rebellion, spent much time with Fidel Castro, and in January 1967 published *Revolution in the Revolution?* in Havana. In April 1967 Debray went to Bolivia as a correspondent for the Mexican weekly *Sucesos*. He was arrested by the Bolivian police while traveling under his own name and in civilian clothes. He was charged with aiding guerrilla insurrectionists active in Bolivia, thought to have been led by Che Guevara. Debray was sentenced to thirty years' imprisonment, but was released in 1970.